THE
GRAND
ILLUSION

THE
GRAND
ILLUSION

LOVE, LIES, AND
MY LIFE WITH STYX

CHUCK PANOZZO
WITH MICHELE SKETTINO

◢AMACOM

AMERICAN MANAGEMENT ASSOCIATION

NEW YORK • ATLANTA • BRUSSELS • CHICAGO • MEXICO CITY • SAN FRANCISCO
SHANGHAI • TOKYO • TORONTO • WASHINGTON, D.C.

Special discounts on bulk quantities of AMACOM books are
available to corporations, professional associations, and other
organizations. For details, contact Special Sales Department,
AMACOM, a division of American Management Association,
1601 Broadway, New York, NY 10019.
Tel.: 212-903-8316. Fax: 212-903-8083.
E-mail: specialsls@amanet.org
Web site: www.amacombooks.org/go/specialsales
To view all AMACOM titles go to: www.amacombooks.org

This publication is designed to provide accurate and authoritative
information in regard to the subject matter covered. It is sold with the
understanding that the publisher is not engaged in rendering legal,
accounting, or other professional service. If legal advice or other expert
assistance is required, the services of a competent professional person
should be sought.

Library of Congress Cataloging-in-Publication Data

Panozzo, Chuck.
    The grand illusion : love, lies, and my life with Styx / Chuck Panozzo with
Michele Skettino.
        p.   cm.
    Includes index.
    ISBN-13: 978-0-8144-0916-9
    ISBN-10: 0-8144-0916-4
    1. Panozzo, Chuck.   2. Styx (Musical group)   3. Rock musicians—United
States—Biography.   4. Gay musicians—United States—Biography.   I. Skettino,
Michele.   II. Title.

ML419.P385A3   2007
782.42166092—dc22
[B]   2007001190

Printing number

10   9   8   7   6   5   4   3   2   1

CONTENTS

Introduction   1

I: GROWING UP CHUCK   5

CHAPTER ONE: Something's Different   7
CHAPTER TWO: Music—The Great Escape   19
CHAPTER THREE: An Unlikely Detour   29
CHAPTER FOUR: The Original Boy Band   39

II: PLAYIN' IN A TRAVELING BAND   53

CHAPTER FIVE: The Wooden Nickel Years   55
CHAPTER SIX: Almost Famous   77
CHAPTER SEVEN: Hey Now, You're a Rock Star   85

III: FREE-FALLING   101

CHAPTER EIGHT: Breaking Up Is Hard to Do   103
CHAPTER NINE: And Now for the Bad News   113

CONTENTS

IV: I'VE GOT A SECRET 133

CHAPTER TEN: The Worst of Times 135
CHAPTER ELEVEN: HIV Ain't for Sissies 159
CHAPTER TWELVE: A Message from a Friend 171
CHAPTER THIRTEEN: Will the Real Chuck Please Stand Up 181

V: ILLUSIONS SHATTERED 191

CHAPTER FOURTEEN: Ready for Love 193
CHAPTER FIFTEEN: Rewriting Happily Ever After 201
CHAPTER SIXTEEN: Faces of Victory 209

EPILOGUE: LESSONS LEARNED 221

ACKNOWLEDGMENTS

Chuck: I would like to thank above all my partner, Tim, for his enthusiastic support for this project. Also, I'd like to thank Michele Skettino for bringing my words to the written page. A big debt of gratitude too to my friends Steven Rice and David Morganlander, who first planted the seed in me to tell my story. Thanks, guys. I'd also like to acknowledge my parents, my twin John, and my sister and her family—there would be no story of my life without them. I must also mention my cousins, who kept my spirit alive during difficult times. Thanks too for the strength, love, and laughter of my lifelong friends Michael Cymbala, Richard, Donna, my college friends Jan, Joe, and Richard, as well as Michele M., MJ, RJ, Gary, Jamie, Dylan Rice, Ron, and Bob. I'd also like to thank the wonderfully supportive Tommy and Jeanne Shaw, and the members of Styx, both past and present, including the road crew. I cannot forget the exceptional medical team at NorthStar, who gave me back my life. And, of course, my babies, Valentino, Max, and Mia, whose love is unconditional.

Michele: Many thanks to my friends David Morganlander and Steve Rice, who fortuitously met Chuck and Tim while traveling, became friends, and ultimately brought us all together. Obviously, the universe had plans for us to write a book! During my many visits to Florida to interview Chuck, Dave and Steve graciously shared their home.

Thanks too to my husband Ed, who supported this project from the start, even when I was flying off to Florida and he was stuck back in New York (in the middle of winter). I'd also like to thank Stan Wakefield, who immediately recognized that Chuck had a special story to tell, and said "yes" to a book contract in record time. And thank you to everyone at AMACOM Publishing who enthusiastically embraced this book. Finally, I thank Chuck, who accepted me and opened up to me immediately. When I bought my first Styx album back in the 7th grade, I never would have imagined that one day I'd call Chuck Panozzo a friend. Chuck, you made the experience of writing this book a true pleasure. I am honored that you chose me to tell your story.

THE
GRAND
ILLUSION

INTRODUCTION

Growing up on the infamous South Side of Chicago with my twin brother John, I felt from an early age that somehow I didn't quite fit in. Subsequently, I spent most of my life looking for a place where I belonged. That search took me many places.

Early in my life, one of those places was the seminary. For a year, I spent my days ingesting the teachings of the Catholic faith, hoping that somewhere among the saints and apostles, I would find my place in the world. Needless to say, that didn't work out very well.

So again, I returned to my childhood neighborhood, and as I would continue to do throughout my life, turned to music to give me a sense of belonging. During those moments when I would pick up my guitar, I could lose myself—at least temporarily—in a particularly intense riff, or an especially poignant lyric. It was good.

My love of music began early. My brother John and I formed our first band at the tender age of twelve. A few years later, our neighborhood pal Dennis DeYoung heard us rehearsing through an open basement window, and we became a trio. After a few incarnations and a few more additions, including James Young and John Curulewski—we ultimately became the rock group Styx.

Over the next decade, Tommy Shaw joined our group and Styx went on to become one of the biggest rock bands around. We were the first rock band ever to sell four consecutive triple-platinum albums. To the rest of the world, I'm sure it looked like we were doing great. And in many ways, we were. But as you can imagine, on an arena stage, under blaring lights, in front of thousands of screaming female fans is not the best place for a gay man to work out his issues. During this time, I kept my sexual orientation a deep secret. While I received some support from my family and a few close friends, I didn't feel that I could tell my bandmates or the world at large. The rock scene at that time wasn't the most accepting environment for a gyrating gay rock stud . . . perhaps it still isn't.

Styx broke up in 1984, and took a six-year hiatus before reforming in 1990. As always, I looked forward to getting back to work and escaping into my music for a while. Then, however, reality kicked in big time. In 1991, I was diagnosed with HIV. I still had not made total peace with my sexual orientation, so maybe Life was trying to give me a wake-up call. It certainly succeeded.

During this time, my brother John was also struggling. After several stints in alcohol rehab, his health continued to deteriorate, and John died in 1996. But fate was not through with the Panozzo brothers. Two years later, I was diagnosed with AIDS. Finally, my health forced me to tell my band members about my condition.

Still, it was not until July 2001 that I came out to the world at a Chicago Human Rights Campaign dinner in front of a thousand people, including family and friends. I didn't want to live in denial anymore. I had seen my brother in denial, and he died of addiction. My best friend was in denial about being HIV positive, and he died of AIDS. I didn't want to be that person. I didn't want to be a coward about this thing anymore.

Fortunately, with the advancements in AIDS treatment, my health has improved and I look forward to the next stage of my life. My viral load is now undetectable. But it will never be life as usual. While I still enjoy playing concert dates with Styx, I now spend a lot of my time speaking out on human rights and HIV/AIDS awareness, and taking care of my health, as well as the health of my partner, Tim.

I'm telling my story so that others may learn from my experience.

On the surface, it's the story about one gay man's struggle to come to terms with himself. But it is really about anyone struggling to come to terms with a troubling aspect of his or her life. If I can make one person question why he's hiding his authentic self—or living in any kind of denial—and give him courage to make a change, then I've succeeded. Then my brother and my friend will not have died in vain.

I'll start my story where it all began, back on the streets of south Chicago.

I
GROWING UP
CHUCK

CHAPTER ONE

SOMETHING'S
DIFFERENT

They say that a major part of our adult personalities are formed in the first few years of our lives. Perhaps that explains a lot in my life. My old neighborhood was a place where men were men, and gay men were "fairies." That's what they called us back then. Of course, at the time, I didn't know *what* I was yet. I just knew that I was different.

I was born on the South Side of Chicago in 1948. I was my mother's only son—her pride and joy—for exactly twenty minutes. That's when my twin brother John hit the scene. And though I have no cognizance of his arrival, I'm sure that he came out raising hell, a personality trait that he carried with him throughout his life. And so began the journey of the Panozzo twins.

John and I were not identical twins. In fact, we were far from it in either looks or personality. He was tall and thin, with—to his chagrin—a full head of brown-spiraled curls. I was shorter and huskier with straight hair and a perpetual cowlick. I flaunted my straight-haired genetic luck until the 1970s, when John's fro suddenly became all the rage. My folic superiority was suddenly wiped out with the advent of the afro pick. With respect to personalities, I was always on the reserved side, while John basically said and did what he felt at the moment. We actually made a good match. I could enjoy the fun from the sidelines, egging him on occasionally, but still manage to stay out of trouble and keep a low profile. I used this technique quite effectively to maintain favored-son status.

My life started out much like any other child of first-generation Italian immigrant parents back in 1940s Chicago. My mother's name was Elizabeth and my father's name was Tranquino—a beautiful Etruscan name—but everyone called him Chip. It was easier to spell and easier to explain down at the plant. John and I also had a sister, Emily Jean, who was four years older.

We lived in a tight-knit family in a tight-knit community called Roseland. Within the greater area of south Chicago, the neighborhoods tended to be segregated by nationality. The Irish had their own neighborhood and their own Catholic church. The Italians had their own, the Polish yet another, and so on. All in all, it worked pretty well. There was no hostility among the groups—it was simply the way that the various immigrant groups settled into the city. It was a way for these new arrivals to live the American dream while still retaining a link to their homeland.

Most of the men in our neighborhood worked in the steel mills or in factories. They defined the middle- to lower-middle-class lifestyle. These men were hard workers who unquestioningly went out to provide for their families every day. They had simple tastes and simple joys. They generally owned one pair of good shoes and one suit worn for weddings, funerals, and Sunday mass. They washed their hands before they ate—never more.

The women who married these men spent their days in the home, caring for their children, cooking, and watching daytime television. They rarely worked outside the home. They wore aprons and set their hair in curlers for special occasions. At the time, I was not aware that anyone lived any other way. In fact, I don't think the adults were either. That's probably why it all ran so smoothly.

I spent the first twenty years of my life in this fairly insulated world. And in my earliest days, I have to say that childhood was quite pleasant inside my parents' home. My mother kept us all close at bay and the days were filled with daily rituals and routines that would probably seem foreign to kids today. Throughout the day we watched my mother clean and cook, and heard her talk on the phone to my aunts or over the fences to other neighborhood women. My home, like most others in the neighborhood, had a strong female presence, as the men left early for work and returned at the end of the day exhausted. My own father worked in a steel mill. When he was home on Saturdays it was like a treat for me. He was something of a jack-of-all-trades, and I loved to follow him around the house helping him on various projects.

As a very young boy, I loved doing quiet things, like coloring and drawing. Frequently while I was playing by myself, John was bouncing around the house getting into some kind of trouble. I remember that my sister used to say, "You know, he's *your twin* brother." But I would just sit amidst the chaos calmly drawing my pictures and enjoying the show that John was putting on.

My love of art and the visual world began early. I remember being drawn to beautiful colors from my youngest days. I was especially fascinated with my sister's nail polish. When Jean would paint her fingernails, I begged her to let me paint mine too. I think she thought it was more amusing than odd, so she would let me use her nail polish, giving me advice on how to keep the color neat and warning me not to spill it or mom would kill us both.

Staring down at my pink and red fingertips, even a five-year-old thinks, "Hmmm. John's not doing this. The other little boys don't seem to be doing this. I wonder why."

Around this time, I began to recognize that something about me was a little bit different. Within my own household, no one really noticed that I wasn't quite like the other children. After all, Emily was older and John was not exactly your typical five-year-old. If my parents were worried about any of their children, it would have been John. He was a handful and demanded the bulk of their attention. When I started school and had more interaction with other kids, that's when my differences became even clearer—at least to me.

I never really jelled with the other neighborhood kids. The boys were always roughhousing. The girls had their own idea of fun. And I couldn't relate to either. I didn't like playing with dolls, but I didn't like getting dirty. I enjoyed drawing more than I liked playing baseball. Of course, at the age of five, who knew why? I just knew that I didn't quite fit in. In school, especially on the playground, I always felt anxious. For one thing, I wasn't very athletic. I'm sure this had to do with my lack of interest in sports, coupled with the very sheltered way in which I was raised.

My father sometimes encouraged John and me to take an interest in sports, but my mother always objected. She didn't want us to get hurt. My mother had irrational fears about almost every situation or activity that could possibly harm herself or her loved ones. Running, driving, jumping, swimming—the normal activities of life—all set her heart pounding, and as her children, we were meant to fear them too. John, being a typical little boy, often fought her on this. Sometimes he would get away with joining a sports team here or there, but in the end my mother's complaining usually won out.

I suppose this can be traced back to her childhood. My mother experienced a lot of tragedies growing up. Her brother passed away as a child and two of her sisters almost died of rheumatic fever. Because of this, she was always afraid that something would happen to her own children. Of course, there's a difference between motherly love and "smotherly love," which John and I eventually started to call it. I know that my mother did the best job that she could and that her motivation was good. It probably wasn't the best way to raise children, but does anyone ever get it entirely right? One irony that still makes me chuckle is that even though my mother never let John or I go near the sports fields, we ended up visiting more football stadiums and baseball fields than most people in America—Styx sang the national anthem at all of them!

When it came time to go to elementary school, my parents decided to send John and me to Catholic school. That's where all the Catholic families who could afford it would send their kids. My parents didn't have much money, but they felt that education was so important that they managed to send all of their children to parochial school. That is where I had my first experience with bullies. I'm not only talking about the other kids. I'm including the older, habited variety.

Like all the Catholic school children back then, we were taught by nuns. These supposedly Mary-like women would hit us with rulers and even punch us with their fists. You had to wonder—did Mary really beat the hell out of Jesus like this? Of course, as kids, we were often too intimidated to tell our parents. And if we did tell, the parents often turned a blind eye. You didn't mess with the nuns, and parents often rationalized that somehow their kids must have done something to deserve the abuse.

John got it particularly hard because he was such a rambunctious kid. Today, I'm sure he would be diagnosed with some sort of learning disability or a form of hyperactivity, but back then he was just deemed a troublemaker. And the nuns didn't have much patience for trouble-makers. There were so many times when John was on the receiving end of their wrath.

I vividly remember one day in particular. School had just been dismissed for the afternoon. John and I and some other kids were still filtering off the schoolyard. One of the few lay teachers was also stand-ing outside and realized that she had forgotten something on her desk. She asked John if he would mind running back inside to get it for her. Once the doors of the school were shut, you were never supposed to go back in, but John did as he was asked. With the rest of the kids on the playground watching, he started to open the big wooden door. Suddenly, a black-clothed arm reached out, grabbed his jacket and yanked him inside. We stood in awe, staring at the doors. Every few seconds, we heard banging noises and saw the doors rattle back and forth. A few minutes later, the doors reopened and the same black-clothed arm threw John back out onto the pavement.

Scenes like this repeated themselves in various incarnations throughout most of our childhood. They must have hurt John, but rather than show it, he developed a tough exterior and a great sense of humor. This made him very popular with the other kids despite his troubles at school. I, on the other hand, was having a harder time fitting in. While John's struggles were with the nuns, mine were with the other kids. Children seem to have an instinctive ability to seek out the weakest among them. Unfortunately, that was usually me.

I was teased mercilessly on a number of different fronts. I was teased about the way that I threw a ball. I was teased about the way that I ran. And probably the most hurtful, I was teased about the way that I talked. My voice was high as a kid, and I suppose a bit effeminate, even among the prepubescent set. I still remember a boy shouting to me, "You sound like a girl. You talk like a fairy."

I didn't even know what a fairy was—outside of the Walt Disney variety—but I was smart enough to know that it wasn't good. That one comment drove me even further into my shell, and during my elementary school days I rarely spoke, for fear of someone else calling me that name again. Looking back, it's ironic to realize that my silence and sense of shame about being gay started before I even knew what the word meant.

Fortunately, when you have a twin, you have an instant friend. While I was always intimidated and would back off rather than stand up for myself, John was always the tough one. I know that John heard the comments that the other kids said about me—we were in the same class. But we never talked about it. In his own way, though, John looked out for me. One day, a couple of older kids surrounded me on the playground and knocked off my baseball cap. My brother saw them and came running over to the boys, shouting, "If you ever do that to my brother again I'm going to punch you in the mouth."

Sure enough, the next day, the same boy knocked off my cap, looking back at my brother the whole time. John didn't hesitate. Despite the difference in their size, he lunged at the boy and punched him in the mouth. There was a little bit of blood, both on the kid's mouth and my brother's fist—and the boy started crying, "I have braces—what do think you're doing! You're in trouble . . ."

My brother walked closer to him and looked up at the boy's bleeding mouth. I thought he was going to apologize. That's what I would have done.

Then I heard John say, "If you ever do anything to my brother again, I'll punch you even harder." That's when I knew that my brother would always have my back. That was very cool.

Exposure to constant negativity and teasing in your early years is no way to start out life. Unfortunately, I imagine many a gay child still has the same experience that I did all those years ago. Of course, a lot of the negative messages that you receive are subliminal. But every child, especially a sensitive one, has the instinctive ability to interpret exactly what a snicker between classmates really means, and to somehow know when the whispering is about you. You also instinctively figure out that even though you have no idea why, your classmates are right: you are different. For a young child, it's like knowing that you have a secret, but not knowing what it is. It's heart wrenching.

One day when I was about nine years old, I figured out what that secret was. During the summer, I had made an awkward turn on my bicycle and ended up with a double compound leg fracture that put me in a huge plaster cast for almost four months. That injury actually continued to limit my physical activity for many years. I suppose this reconfirmed to my mother that all forms of outdoor recreation were indeed dangerous and to be avoided at all costs. When the school year began, I was still on crutches, maneuvering as best I could around the school's staircases and narrow hallways. Clearly, universal design was not high on the priority list for Chicago's parochial schools in the 1950s.

During one of my first weeks back to school, the principal walked into the classroom and said, "Charles, we're going to have a fire drill today. During the drill, I've asked one of the eighth grade boys to pick you up and carry you downstairs."

I said, "OK, Sister," and thought, "Fire drill, cool."

When the time came, the designated eighth grade boy came to the classroom door. As he began to walk toward me, I thought "Wow!"

Ding, ding, ding. The fire alarms weren't the only bells going off. I was nine; he was twelve—it was like James Dean walking toward me.

In that modulating voice unique to adolescent boys, he said, "I'm going to pick you up now, Charles. I want you to grab me around the neck real tight so I don't drop you."

"No problem," I said.

When the fire drill was over, he brought me back to my classroom. The principal came in to ask me how it went.

I said, "Fine, Sister. Can we have another fire drill tomorrow?" That's when the puzzle was complete.

After my experience during the fire drill, I suddenly knew why I didn't want to hang out with the girls, and why I didn't fit in with the boys. I liked boys the way that most boys liked girls. Of course, at that point, I had no idea what being gay meant. My life was very shielded and no one ever talked about sex—period. Our parents' thinking was, "Oh, they'll find out in due time. It will just happen." This was the way most people handled the topic back then. Of course, it usually "happened" in all the wrong ways—whether on the playground or in the backseat of some unknowing parent's car—hence the rash of forced marriages and an amazing number of ten-pound "premature" babies. "Imagine," the new grandmothers would say, "Such a big baby and two months early!"

In this fantastical environment of magical babies and virgin brides, certainly no one ever talked about homosexual sex. No one even said the word "gay" in 1950s Chicago, especially in my neck of the woods. I had the feeling that I was alone in the universe and that I might have to visit another planet to find someone who understood what I was feeling. The only clue I had that there were other people out there like me came from snippets of conversation that I would pick up from the grown ups around the dinner table. Anyone suspected of being gay would be brought up in the context of a joke. The men would refer to the "fruits" or "faggots" and the women would giggle about the "queers."

Of course, we didn't even know many men back in the old neighborhood who fit this description. I do remember two. They were friends of the family who worked in two stereotypical professions: one was a hairdresser and the other was a florist. I was always a little bit curious about these men, who like me, seemed a little bit different. One day, my mother and I were watching television, and we saw the man who was the hairdresser on one of the local talk shows. I was amazed. Back in the 1950s it was a huge deal for anyone to be on television—especially someone from our neighborhood. My mother and I watched the segment, and I thought, "That's cool, he must be very successful."

A few minutes later, one of my relatives called and asked, "Did you see the queer on television?"

I knew then from this simple remark that no matter how nice or how successful this man seems, it didn't matter. He would always be less of a person in the eyes of most of the people in my world.

We also knew a very popular caterer who was rumored to be gay. He catered a lot of weddings and parties in our neighborhood. Once John and I began playing in a band, we often worked the same events and got to know him pretty well. He was a nice man. Years later, I got to know his partner after meeting him in bar. After all those years, I had confirmation that he was indeed gay. So the rumors were true. Of course, I never told anybody. It none of their business and the questions would have arisen, "Where did you meet his partner? What were you doing in a gay bar?" The sad part is that he was one of the first men to contract HIV in the early days of the disease. When he passed away, I remember reading in his obituary that he died of an unknown cause.

These experiences taught me early on to adopt the "don't ask, don't tell" policy. I felt that I had a terrible secret, and although I may have wanted to talk about it desperately—to ask questions, to find out why—the consequences of doing so back then were severe. Although it probably seems unbelievable to young people today, back in the 1950s, parents who thought that their children might have gay tendencies would often send them away to military school, or even psychiatric hospitals, to "cure" them. At this time, the American Psychiatric Association still listed homosexuality as a mental illness. It wasn't removed from the list until 1973.

In the 1950s, psychiatric hospitals would sometimes use aversion therapy to try to convert homosexual men back to the "straight and narrow." These poor men, often just boys, would be shown images of naked, or attractive men, and simultaneously given drugs that caused nausea and vomiting. Most men would end up feigning their "cure" simply to escape this abuse. The cure generally lasted until they could get away from their families. Or in the saddest cases, these men were scared into hiding their sexual orientation for the rest of their lives.

This was the kind of ignorance about homosexuality that surrounded me growing up. Unfortunately, my experience was not atypical. Many young men and women growing up gay at that time experienced the same type of ignorance and prejudice. Of course, I don't think that my own parents would have sent me away, or beaten me, if I told them about the feelings that I was having, but I also don't think that they could have accepted it or understood it. They were smart people, but very entrenched in their world. Catholic, first-generation Italian-Americans in our lower-middle-class neighborhood didn't want to hear about such things—especially not from their children.

So telling my parents was out. Telling my teachers—the nuns— was really out. And telling anyone my own age—even John—seemed too risky at the time. Unfortunately, there was no place else to turn for support. There was no neutral source of information that would have allowed me to understand my feelings and make sense of them in the context of the larger world outside of my sheltered neighborhood.

Back then, homosexuality was not something written about in the mainstream media. There were no newspaper or magazine stories profiling gay men or women. There were no books covering gay issues in the library. There were no cable shows called "The L Word" or "Queer as Folk." There was no Internet. The hottest movie couple around wasn't Jake Gyllenhaal and Heath Ledger; it was Doris Day and Rock

Hudson (with the irony not yet realized). I had no way of looking outside of Roseland, and therefore had no role models and no way of figuring out who and what I was all about. I was walking through the jungle without a guide.

Of course, when I first realized my attraction to boys, I was much too young to act on any of my feelings. The only thing causing all my internal turmoil was simply a fleeting feeling of attraction toward a boy. But simply having those feelings made me think that somehow I had already done something wrong. I must be bad. Obviously, I was brought up in a devout Catholic household, and we had been learning the teachings of Catholicism and listening to priests' ominous sermons as long as I could remember. In fact, John and I were altar boys all through my elementary school years. Growing up Catholic is hard enough for an adolescent boy even if you're straight, but growing up gay? Talk about guilt.

One day when I was about ten years old, while sitting up on the altar during mass, I heard the priest talking about "those men who don't get married." His words were deliberately vague, but his tone said it all. There was repulsion in his voice. As the sermon continued, he went on to say how selfish "those men" were, and warned that they would all go to hell. Even though I was only ten, I realized that he was talking about me.

CHAPTER TWO

MUSIC—
THE GREAT ESCAPE

The words of that priest found their way into my soul. I couldn't see the fairness in being condemned to hell simply because I was different. Yet a sense of shame and guilt began to build in my ten-year-old brain that stayed with me for most of my adult life.

I developed a theory. If I didn't call too much attention to myself, I might slip by unnoticed. So, when the kids teased that I ran like a girl, I stopped going out onto the playground. When another one of the boys said that I sounded like a faggot, I stopped talking. I tried to become invisible. Slowly, my contact with the outside world became increasingly limited, and I was living my own isolated existence with few friends outside of my family.

Fortunately, my family was large enough and lively enough to provide a lot of entertainment. Christmas, Easter, birthdays or christenings—it didn't matter. Italians love a celebration. My whole family—aunts, uncles, cousins, sister, brother—would gather together at someone's house. There would be lots of food and drinking, and music—always music. My great-uncles from Italy would drag out their instruments from the Old Country, and everyone would sing and dance. There were accordions and guitars. One of my uncles used to play an instrument made out of the bladder of a sheep. When you're a kid and you see an old man playing a song on a sheep bladder, believe me, it's intriguing.

I was always fascinated by the music. I would listen intently and watch everyone singing along to Italian lyrics even though I had no idea what the words meant. At the same time, John was appreciating the music in his own way. As a young kid, he was constantly banging on anything he could find—pots, pans, furniture, or other people—it didn't matter. He had a natural rhythm that seemed to radiate throughout his body. Fortunately, we had someone in our lives who spotted our musical inclinations and made an offer that would change our lives.

My Uncle Tony was a professional musician. When John and I were about seven or eight years old, Uncle Tony was long out of the service and living in Chicago. He and my mother were very close. When my parents first married, my own father had been recruited into the service during World War II. He was sent overseas, leaving my mother back home with a young daughter, my sister Emily Jean. Not wanting to live alone, and to save money while my father was away, my mother moved back home to live with my grandparents and a house full of brothers. My sister Emily, "the baby," became a focal point for the whole family, including Tony. So when he eventually went into the service, then returned home, he seemed to have a special connection with my mother's family. He grew very close to John and me. Uncle Tony loved to fish, and so did my father, so sometimes we would all go out on the lake and fish for trout.

Spending so much time together, it's not surprising that he picked up on the fact that John and I were drawn to music. One day, he said to my parents, "The boys are getting older. They should be playing an instrument. Let me give them lessons."

My parents would have never asked him to do this, but since he offered, they agreed to let us begin drum lessons in my Uncle Tony's basement.

Uncle Tony was a very interesting man who had seen a bit more of the world than some of my other relatives. He worked as a drummer at Chicago's famous Pump Room for over eighteen years. The Pump Room was a very upscale restaurant in Chicago's Gold Coast—an area quite different from Roseland. In its heyday, the Pump Room was a magnet for Hollywood celebrities. Bette Davis, Humphrey Bogart and Lauren Bacall, Robert Wagner and Natalie Wood, and Frank Sinatra were all said to be regulars. It was always fun to imagine my uncle mingling in these circles, and he would sometimes entertain the family with stories of who he saw and what they said or did that night.

Uncle Tony was also a painter, with a studio in his house. This was especially fascinating to me because he was the only adult that I knew who shared my love of colors and paints. He was clearly an amateur painter, but he did win a local award here or there, which impressed the family considerably. Uncle Tony gave our family some bragging rights, and through him, I got a glimpse of a whole new world outside of Roseland. When we would walk through the house for our music lessons, the paints and easels in his studio intrigued John and me. Then, going down into the basement where he kept his drum sets and stereo equipment, we were wide-eyed at the shiny drums and cymbals. We couldn't wait to start making noise.

Uncle Tony introduced me to the world of music, and I couldn't have been more excited. Every week, John and I began going over to his house and learning to play the drums. John was a natural. He had an innate rhythm, and the instrument seemed to fit with his personality as well. The drums offered a perfect outlet for a hyperactive child; he could bang and smash to his heart's content.

After a couple of months, we all realized that John was catching on a lot faster than I was. Without even trying, he could beat the sticks in perfect rhythm. I would practice for hours on end and still couldn't quite keep the beat. It became apparent rather quickly that my brother John was a great drummer—and I was horrible. Frustrated, I decided that drums weren't for me. Let John be the drummer. My uncle, a wise man, didn't argue. But rather than turn me away from music altogether, he suggested an alternative—the six-string rhythm guitar. That worked out a bit better. I remember the first time I held the guitar. It felt more natural to me right from the start. So it was decided; John would be the drummer and I would play guitar.

Both my uncle and my parents were very encouraging to John and me about our music. My parents didn't have much money, but they always found a way to give us music lessons and buy us our instruments. I suppose they felt that it kept us off the streets and out of trouble. In our neighborhood, it wasn't uncommon for many of the kids, especially boys, to perpetually get into trouble. But once we started to play instruments, in our free time we were always at home practicing or out taking lessons. That made my mother especially happy. Not only were we making our parents happy, but also we loved our newfound hobby.

John, in particular, began to excel. He was a natural musician. It took me a little longer to master the guitar than it took John to master the drums, but around the time I turned twelve, I could play rhythm guitar pretty well. Since, in a band, the rhythm guitarist and drummer work closely together, John and I formed the Panozzo rhythm section. It seemed like the perfect musical combo for twin boys.

As twins, we always seemed to attract attention anyway. But now, with our newly found musical skills, we couldn't walk into a room without causing a stir. We were always ready to perform at a moment's notice, whether it be singing or playing. Some kids have to be begged to sing a song or recite a poem. You didn't have to ask us twice.

John always found a way to make it hysterical too. He was always the clown—even if I was the only one who got the joke. There is one memory of John that I'll never forget. Every year, our church held a summertime festival in honor of St. Alexander. After mass, the men of the parish would carry a statue of St. Alexander on a wooden platform out of the church and into the streets. A procession would follow. The men would carry the statue up and down the streets past the parishioners' houses. When the stature would pass by, women and little girls in white dresses would shoot off fireworks to ward off evil spirits and pin money to the stole around the statue's neck. (Not too pagan, was it?) The church would end up collecting thousands of dollars on the statue by the time the procession was over. Leading the march was a little band of mostly Italian immigrants who would all play marches out of tune. And, of course, the backbone of their band was the drummer.

One year they needed a new drummer for the processional. They were all so old that maybe their former drummer couldn't make the walk anymore. I'm not sure. For whatever the reason, they ended up asking my brother if he would be the new drummer for the festival. John was thrilled. This is exciting for a kid. Essentially, there was a moment of religion, then bacchanalia. There was even a carnival at the end of the day. So John learned all the songs, including the main marching tune, *L'Inno di Mameli*, the Italian national anthem.

When the day came, John was out playing with the band, marching through the streets. He did a great job. My mother and father, and all my aunts and uncles were so proud of him. But then he started to get tired. It was a hot day and he didn't have much of an attention span even under the best of conditions. Basically, he wanted to finish the procession and go home. As we followed along, I noticed that each song he played was getting a little bit faster.

After a few more stanzas, the old guys were huffing and puffing and yelling, "Johnny, a-slow it a-down. Slow it a-down."

But John just kept on playing as if he didn't even hear them. I knew that John was getting such a kick out of this. He was killing these guys. I was laughing from the sidelines. Little did they know, cute little Johnny who everyone thought was so precocious was actually the devil. This was the kind of innocent act that John would pull for all his stunts. Often, I was the only one who realized what was going on. John wasn't innocent at all. He knew exactly what he was doing and he loved every minute of it.

By the time we were teenagers, John and I had graduated from Uncle Tony's basement and started taking lessons at a music school in our neighborhood. We were in the minority at music school in terms of instrument selection. In the early 1960s, accordions were the most popular instruments in Italian neighborhoods. Every Italian mother wanted her son to play the accordion and forced them into lessons. I guess it was cheaper than the piano and just as fun at parties.

Once a week at our music school, all the accordions would get together to perform. John and I—as the sole rhythm section—were asked to perform as well. There we were, the Panozzo twins, keeping the beat for twenty-five preteen accordion players of varying degrees of competence. I can only imagine what we sounded like, but I looked forward to performing with the accordions each week. Honestly, I loved it. For the first time, I wasn't being judged or singled out in a bad way. In fact, we were something of the stars of the accordion set. Some might say we were merely King of the Geeks, but nonetheless it felt good.

It is not an understatement to say that music was changing my life. Once I started to play an instrument, suddenly I felt that I had something of value to contribute. Guitar was my thing. Now, in my own head, I was someone beyond the little, fag queer on the playground. I had a talent that I could use to win acceptance. I didn't have to compete in sports. I didn't have to be the best-looking guy. All I had to do was dive into my music.

John had caught the bug too. We loved to perform and wanted to start our own band. But in order for us to break out on our own, we needed someone to provide the melody. So we asked one of the better accordion players if he was interested in playing with us. His name was Wayne, and together we formed our first little trio. The three of us would practice for hours in my parents' basement, fueled by a few wins in some local talent competitions. But alas, eventually Wayne's interest waned, coinciding with the onset of puberty, and once again we were left a twosome. Fortunately, fate would send someone else to our door.

Soon after Wayne left us, John and I were practicing together on a hot summer day in my parents' basement, our makeshift studio. The street that we lived on was typical for our neighborhood, with little wood-framed houses on small lots of land. No one had air conditioners, so in the summertime with all of the windows open, you could hear everything that went on in the houses. On this particular day, the sound of our instruments drifted out of the window screens and down the street.

When John and I broke from a song, something caught our eye in the basement window. There was a head peering in at us. A boy a couple of years older than us was staring in. We recognized him from the neighborhood. Eventually, he spoke.

"Hey, you guys sound pretty good."

We thanked him, and started playing again. But he didn't go away. After a minute he said, "You know I play too. Maybe I could come over tomorrow and sit in with you."

We needed a third anyway, so we said sure.

The next day, Dennis DeYoung joined our trio. The instrument that he played at the time was, not surprisingly, the accordion. But as soon as he started playing we knew that there was something different about him. He was young, but he played like an adult. He could run rings around anyone, regardless of their age. And even then he had a head of crazy rock-star curls that somehow made him stand out from the crowd and demanded attention. We were on to something here. Quickly, we forgot Wayne and welcomed Dennis to the trio.

For the rest of the summer, the three of us practiced regularly. We would alternate between our house and his house, which was only a few blocks away. Since it was summer, sometimes we would sit outside on the porch, playing and singing. Since the houses in our neighborhood were so close together, all the neighbors heard everything. Maybe those were simpler times, but unbelievably, nobody seemed to mind the noise. In fact, they even seemed to like it. In the evenings, some of the neighbors would come out on their stoops and ask, "Are you boys going to play for us tonight?"

We loved the attention. Our parents enjoyed it too, and you could see the pride on their faces when we would entertain the neighbors.

In the beginning we always played songs from a huge songbook called *The Black Book* that had about 2,000 songs in it. The songs were classics like "Moon River" and "Good Night Ladies." Eventually, the three of us learned to play two hours of American standards. That was our goal. If you could fill up two hours, you could start getting jobs.

By January of the next year, about six months after we started playing together, we got our first gig. It was a New Year's Eve party in the neighborhood. Of course, none of us could drive yet, so our parents drove us to the party and picked us up. I guess we did a good job, because word got around and we began to get more bookings. Parties, christenings, graduations—we even started getting a few weddings. We would put on our little suits, pile our instruments into our parents' car, and do our thing. For thirteen-year-olds, we thought we were pretty damn cool.

When John and I were fourteen, we started at a Catholic coed high school. Dennis, who was two years older, was already in a different high school. By this time, we were quite popular on the wedding/party circuit. So, when we heard that our school was having a dance, naturally we thought that we should be the ones to play at it. John and I approached one of sisters at the school who was in charge of the extracurricular events. We told her that we had a band and volunteered to play the upcoming dance. She was a very nice woman and agreed on the spot to let us perform. This was going to be our first performance for kids our own age, and we were very excited.

The three of us got to the gym early and set up. We were nervous, but confident, since we had been performing quite a bit over the past year. Eventually, the kids started filtering in. We stayed hidden next to the makeshift stage, until one of the nuns signaled that it was time. The lights dimmed a bit and we walked onto the stage. Everyone applauded—eager and a little curious to hear how we were going to sound. I don't think they were used to seeing their classmates performing at dances—especially two little freshman brothers.

Dennis made a few introductions, and we started to play. How can I say this? It sucked. Looking out at the kids, I could see their smiling faces begin to grow quizzical. I don't really know what we were playing—it could have been anything from "Blue Moon" to "Someone to Watch Over Me," but whatever it was, it wasn't winning over the crowd. It was 1962. Elvis Presley, the Supremes, the Kingston Trio, and Ricky Nelson were some of the names of the day. Cole Porter and Frank Sinatra—not so much.

The kids began to look around at each other, as if to ask, "Are they serious?" Then, their smiles began to return—but not in a good way. It was a disaster. We played a few more songs, but the crowd grew slimmer, as the kids began filtering out of the gym to smoke and flirt, and presumably decide where they were going to go now that the dance was a bust. Eventually, we came down off the stage. We were humiliated. The sister who had given us the gig knew how bad we felt. She ended up giving us some great advice that changed the course of our band, and you could even say, the course of our lives.

She said, "You guys were great. It's just the music you were playing. These kids want to hear rock 'n roll. That's what you need to start playing."

And she was right. At fourteen years old, we were an old-time wedding band, but no one was getting married in the gym that night.

It just goes to show the tremendous impact—either for good or bad—that the words of adults can have on young people. If that nun had had a different reaction, I don't know what would have happened to our trio. But we took her words to heart. Not many rock bands start out by getting the best advice of their careers from a nun, but if you think about it, it's not a bad source of Providence. At least it wasn't for us.

From that night on, the three of us began listening to the radio and trying to replicate the songs that we heard. Some of the big artists in 1962 were Chubby Checker, Neil Sedaka, Jerry Lee Lewis, and Elvis

Presley. We learned them all. Eventually, we were confidant enough to return to the school for a talent contest. This time, we ruled. The kids loved us, and we ended up taking second place. First place went to some awful opera singer who all the nuns thought had a "beautiful voice." We didn't care. We were on our way. And, incidentally, I don't think that opera singer ever went triple platinum.

CHAPTER THREE

AN UNLIKELY DETOUR

Music found its way into my life in another way as well. Every Sunday John and I would stand in the wings of St. Anthony of Padua's Church waiting to serve as Knights of the Altar for the 12:15 late-morning mass—generally the most coveted time slot among all the other altar boys. I could hardly wait for the show to begin each week. We would stand in the back of the church looking out at all the heads filling the pews. In those days, the women had to cover their heads inside the churches, and most wore little lace doilies pinned to the back of their heads. The men wore shirts and ties. Eventually, the organ music would swell—our cue to follow the priest down the long aisle wearing our little vestments to take our place beside the altar.

Talk about great theatre. All we needed was a nun in the balcony yelling, "Lights, camera, action!"

The rituals and ceremony of the Catholic faith are extraordinary. Everyone gets to wear costumes. There's singing. Each participant has a role to play. There are lines to remember and rehearsals to attend. Participating in the Catholic mass was what I consider to be my first experience in the theater, and I loved it.

I suppose that is part of the reason why, at fifteen years old, I made a dramatic decision that would have a profound impact on the rest of my life and alter my relationship with the Catholic Church forever. The summer before my sophomore year of high school, I decided to join the seminary. Why would a gay teenager want to enter the Catholic priesthood—the very institution that I heard with my own ears condemning me to eternity in hell? It's complicated. I believe part of my motivation was to prove that they were wrong—that I was a "good boy" after all despite the feelings that I was having toward other boys. I also think that despite the solace that I was beginning to feel by being part of our three-man band, I was still seeking a place where I truly felt a sense of belonging and affirmation.

Boy, was I in for a shock! Looking back from an adult's perspective, my disillusionment certainly is not surprising. How could anyone at the age of fifteen make such a profound decision about how he wants to live the rest of his life? How could such a young person understand the implications of a complete vow of chastity before he even understands his own sexual feelings? And in my case, how could a *gay* fifteen-year-old commit to a life that in essence condemned homosexuality? To their credit, my parents discouraged me from going into the seminary. My mother, in particular, was very upset to see me go. But, as a typical teenager, I was insistent. I told them that this was what I wanted to do, and there was little they could do to stop me.

In September of 1963, I entered St. Augustine Seminary as a second-year student. The program was a seminary high school that was supposed to be the beginning of a boy's "formation" to become a priest. Back then, the church thought that the earlier it got you and started brainwashing you, the better. Of course now I believe even the Catholic Church recognizes that this is a mistake. So many men in those days went into the seminary too soon, before they got to experience life, which contributes to all the stories about Father So-and-So fooling around with the church receptionist, or much worse.

It sounds clichéd, but most of the Catholic immigrants—especially the Italian and Irish families in my neighborhood—wanted at least one of their sons to become a priest. By the end of eighth grade, it wasn't uncommon to hear a mother saying, "Little Johnny is going to be a priest." It was really sad, because what did Little Johnny know at that age? What did I know? Everything that I thought it was, it wasn't.

I had a very unrealistic view of the seminary. I didn't think it would be a soft place, but I did think that it would be a place where you would learn and do acts of kindness and generosity. Perhaps having been the target of so much teasing and unkindness in my early years, this is what attracted me to the seminary. But essentially, it turned out to be a boarding school for incorrigible young men. Many of them were from rich families whose parents thought this would be a good way to get them back on the straight and narrow. Or, they were from large families whose parents were looking for a place to ship off a child or two.

I found the priests no better. The fathers didn't commingle with the seminarians so that we could learn from them or use them as mentors. In fact, they didn't even commingle with each other. No one seemed to like each other. When we would have meals, all the priests would sit in one room and the seminarians would sit in another, separated by five-foot-tall glass doors. When the seminarians would get too loud, one of the priests would stand and peer over the glass until we quieted down.

Like the nuns in parochial school, the priests in the seminary were no strangers to physical abuse. Punching, slapping, and beatings were not unusual. I remember one priest in particular who taught Latin. He used to walk up and down the aisles cracking kids with his belt the way that someone would slap another guy with a towel at the gym. You could hear his footsteps walking up and down the aisle, never knowing whether this would be your day to feel the belt on your back. You could actually see on his face the great pleasure that he got from abusing these young boys in this way. He was really a sick person.

Some of these priests had not completed any formal training in teaching and had no real desire to help children learn. Years later when I was in college, I saw this same priest in the parking lot. He told me that he was there to take a few teaching courses. I can only hope that someone stepped in to discipline this man and change the way that he treated his students. But it's difficult to imagine that he was capable of that kind of dramatic change.

Here's a typical day in the seminary. We were up at 6 a.m. You couldn't speak from the time that you woke up until you took a shower (the water was always freezing), got dressed in a shirt and tie, attended mass, and took your seat at breakfast. Once everyone was seated, one of the priests would ring a bell and break the Great Silence. Then, you could say the first words of the day. We would have a little free time and then start our classes. Around midday, we broke for lunch, where I took turns with the other boys serving the meal. All of the seminarians were assigned certain chores, and my assignment was serving as a waiter during meals. Then, we went to afternoon classes. After school, we had a little more free time, then dinner, then study time. Bedtime was at 9 p.m., when the Great Silence would begin again. When I say we had "free time" I use the words loosely. We were allowed no television, no radio, no newspapers or magazines. We were never allowed off campus. In short, we were not allowed any outside influences to interfere with the teachings of the fathers.

We didn't even break the "no news" rule for major historical events. I was in the seminary when John F. Kennedy was assassinated in November of 1963. I remember the day clearly. The headmaster called us all in to a general assembly. None of us could understand why we were being pulled out of classes in the middle of the day. This kind of thing never happened. As we gathered, I remember looking at the faces of the adults in the room. They all looked very serious and very shaken. Finally, the head father spoke. "I have some sad news. The president has been shot. We're dismissing you for the rest of the day."

That was it. We were sent back to our rooms with no more information, no details, and no way of making sense of what we had just heard.

The news of Kennedy's death stunned me. It seemed like everything changed that day. A sense of innocence was taken away from an entire country. I, like the rest of the world, had been captivated by the young, beautiful couple who had become the country's First Couple. They were so unlike the only other presidential couple that I could remember, Dwight and Mamie Eisenhower. But, unlike the rest of the country, which watched the events unfold on television over the next week and could grieve together as a nation, we were kept in the dark. I don't understand why the seminarians felt that they had to keep such a close guard on minds. It wasn't the Middle Ages anymore. I just know that it was extremely isolating.

My most vivid memories from the seminary—besides the physical abuse—center on a small group of boys that I met there who I believe were as confused about their sexuality as I was. One of my first encounters with one of these boys came one autumn afternoon.

The campus of the seminary was beautiful. It sat right on the edge of Lake Michigan. I was down by the lake, just sitting on a rock and thinking, when a young man from the freshman class approached me. We made some small talk and then the conversation got a little strange. He started telling me that he often woke up in the morning with erections, and he was upset that this was happening. Apparently some of the other boys in his dorm were teasing him and giving him a hard time about it. He was obviously upset, and I felt bad for him.

"That's normal," I said. "It just means you have to go the bathroom. It happens to all guys."

Back in those days, nobody was given much information about their bodies, so his naivete was not that surprising.

"Those guys who are teasing you are jerks. Don't let it get to you," I said.

He didn't seem to want to end the conservation there.

"Do you think?" he said. "I guess it's normal. But what if it's something else?"

He kept the questions going, hinting that it might be something else. I think he was vulnerable and a bit homesick—and probably a bit curious—and saw something in me that made him want to open up. But I would have none of it.

I said, "I don't want to talk about this anymore," and walked away.

I wasn't ready to go any further or suggest that erections are anything more than physical reactions to bodily functions.

The conversation made me uncomfortable on a number of fronts. This was the first time that any boy had ever even hinted at wanting to talk about feelings that were remotely sexual, and I wasn't ready for it. In addition, I didn't know who might be listening. Even though we were alone, you never knew who might be lurking, and the consequences of this kind of conversation were unthinkable. The priest kept a close watch on us. They didn't want any of the seminarians to form too close a friendship with another boy. If they saw two boys spending too much time together, they would pull them aside individually and ask about their relationship.

So, after that brief encounter, the freshman boy and I went our separate ways. That was one slippery slope that I wanted to avoid. However, I did eventually gravitate toward another group of boys in my own grade who—in my mind—were quite obviously gay. They looked a little different, they spoke a little different. They acted like I did.

Of course, none of us ever talked about our sexuality. We never talked about boys. We never opened up about our feelings. We just hung out together. Somehow that was enough at the time, and all that we were ready for. It was nice to find friends who I felt comfortable with, since most of the boys sent to the school were troubled or troublemaking kids with whom I had little in common. It was also nice to know for the first time that there were other people in the world like me—even if we couldn't talk about it.

I vividly recall one cold Chicago afternoon when these boys and I were huddled into a dorm room enjoying the one hour of free time that we had each day. We were all drinking Tab, since that was the only beverage that was ever stocked in the soda machine. When I first got to the seminary, I thought this was the most disgusting stuff I had ever tasted. But after two months, Tab was the best discovery in the world. I don't know how much caffeine it had in it, but it must have been supercharged.

On this particular afternoon, one of the boys had smuggled in a radio. As I said, this was considered contraband at the seminary. We were all sitting around, talking, getting on our caffeine buzz and listening to the local rock 'n' roll station. All of a sudden, a really good song came on that we all knew. I don't remember what the song was, but before we knew it, one of the boys jumped up and started dancing like a maniac. I also remember that he was the cutest of the bunch, so maybe that's why the rest of us all jumped up as if on cue and joined him. As we were all rocking out, dancing around, I remember thinking, "This is really cool." It was nice to be able to feel so free in front of a group of boys my own age. I had never experienced anything like that before.

We were quite a sight—five fifteen-year-old Catholic schoolboys rocking out and sweating to the beat of a scratchy transistor radio. That has the makings of quite a few fantasies, I'm sure, but I didn't really know about that stuff back then. We must have kept dancing for ten minutes or so, until we all collapsed, laughing and breathless. After a minute or two, the euphoria passed. We sat back, spent, with eyes averted. All the energy and emotion that we had been repressing for so long had been released. But I think all of us had the same thought: we can never do this again.

I wonder what the priests would have said if they had walked in on that scene. Speaking of fantasies, I'm sure some of them would have enjoyed it quite a bit. I don't know of any specific instances of inappropriate behavior toward the boys by the priests, and I hope there were none. But it was such an insulated world with nowhere for the boys to turn for guidance or support. Somehow, I can't help but think that at least some poor boy may have suffered in silence inside those walls.

Today, most of us in the room that afternoon so long ago have come to terms with our sexuality. Some of us are more out than others, but I hope for the most part we have all found peace and acceptance with ourselves.

The seminary didn't allow the students to return home to visit their families. They had to come to us. So, my family would pile in the car and drive up to see me every month. The visits were always kind of stilted. It was almost like visiting inmates. I could always see the confusion in my parents' faces and how much my mother missed me. But they never pressured me to leave. My brother, on the other hand, was more straightforward.

During one of their visits John blurted out, "This place is horrible. Why don't you just come home with us?"

I remember saying that I wish I could, but that I needed to finish what I started. As time went on, however, my feelings began to change. By the end of the school year, sticking it out just wasn't important to me anymore. I wanted out. One of the kinder priests took me aside and asked, "Charles, how are you feeling?"

I said, "Not good." When school was over, my parents came to pick me up and I never looked back.

After I got home, my sister noticed that Sunday mornings didn't have the same cache for me. She said, "You really seem to have changed about church, Chuck."

I said, "Because I see it for what it is."

Sometimes organized religion can help the masses, but in terms of spirituality—saying prayers correctly, or kneeling at the proper time, it's just ritual. And there's more to spirituality than ritual.

I still feel the same way today. I'm not a practicing Catholic. I will still be buried in the ritual of the Catholic Church, but it's not important for me to go to church every Sunday, and I don't believe that I'm damned because I'm gay. I think God made me just like he made everyone else, so I don't think he's going to send me to hell.

I think part of the problem with the issue of gays and the Catholic Church is that gay priests within the church refuse to speak out. It is not uncommon to see a priest in a gay bar. Of course, they wear street clothes and don't publicize what they do for a living, but you can figure it out pretty quickly. These men are simply not being honest with themselves. They are part of a club that requires them to give false credentials in order to get in. I think it is fine for a gay man to have a sincere calling to be a priest. I have no doubt that they can do a great job for their parishioners. But I find hypocrisy in anyone who hangs out in a gay bar on Saturday night, then preaches about the "sin" of homosexuality on Sunday morning.

Many years after my experience at St. Augustine, my friend Michael and I took a drive up to Saugatuck, Michigan to visit a friend. On the way, we passed by the old site of the seminary. It is now a prison. What irony. I said to Michael, "Oh, look! Now the barbed wire is on the outside instead of around our brains."

CHAPTER FOUR

THE ORIGINAL
BOY BAND

After my year in the seminary, I started my junior year in a new, all-boys Catholic high school. John had already gone there for his sophomore year, so basically he was already running the place.

It was 1964, and while I was in the seminary, the Beatles had begun their reign in America. Since we had such limited exposure to radio in the seminary, I had all but missed their debut. But now, I was catching up quickly, and I loved what I heard. I was eager to start playing music again with John and Dennis. There was one hitch though. While I was away, they had asked another boy to join the group and take my place on rhythm guitar. His name was Tom and he wasn't a bad player. I thought, "I'll be damned if some new kid is going to squeeze me out of my band."

I had an idea. By now, the guys were playing all rock 'n' roll music that they were picking up from the radio. They sounded good, but something was missing. I figured out what that was.

I went up to the guys one day at rehearsal and said, "You know, you can't have a decent rock 'n' roll band without a bass. I'm your new bass guitarist."

Of course, I didn't actually know how to play the bass yet, but that was a detail. Obviously John wasn't going to complain—he wanted his brother in the band. Dennis didn't vehemently object to the idea, and Tom was probably just relieved that I wasn't going after his position.

So, it was decided. I would play the electric bass. It was actually a relatively new instrument at the time. If you ever watch the old Elvis Presley movies, all the band scenes still have the regular stand-up basses. But the four-string electric bass guitar was becoming a more recognized part of many of the rock bands in the 1960s. It wasn't that different from rhythm guitar, but it took me a while to get the hang of it. I'm sure this didn't make the other band members very comfortable. With practice though, eventually I got the groove and our little foursome was born.

We went by the name of the Trade Winds. When we would perform, we would wear black suits and long black ties. We looked pretty good for high school kids, and very professional. By this time, after heeding the advice of that mentoring nun back in freshman year, we had successfully made the transition from wedding band to rock 'n' roll band. Our reputation with kids our own age was growing. We would play whatever we heard on the radio. Dennis was able to pick up the melody in a heartbeat, and the rest of us could figure out our parts from there. By this time, Dennis had given up his accordion. It wasn't cool for rock songs, so he taught himself to play the keyboards. He was a natural musician, so the transition for him wasn't difficult.

Since Dennis was two years older than John and I, in the spring of 1965 he graduated from high school. I suppose this could have meant the end of our band. But Dennis decided to go to college locally, so his graduation actually opened up even more opportunities for the Trade Winds. This was one of the first in a string of favorable circumstances that kept propelling our band forward. Looking back, there are so many life changes along the way between grade school and adulthood that could have pulled us apart, it's amazing that none of us ever gave up on the idea of playing in a band. Through college, girlfriends, marriage, jobs, children—John, Dennis, and I never gave up on our dream. I suppose we all hung on for different reasons; but we all agreed that we weren't ready to let it go.

When Dennis enrolled in college in the fall, he made the right connections and managed to get us in to play at college mixers. Many of these college parties were everything that you would expect from the term "frat party." Think *Animal House*. Now think two sixteen-year-old kids in suits. I'm surprised they even let us in the door.

Playing for this somewhat older crowd, as opposed to only at high school dances, made a big difference in our workload. We started to make a name for ourselves around the South Side of Chicago. The invitations to play better gigs for more money started coming in. Right around this time, another band with the name Trade Winds had a hit song that started to attract some attention, so to avoid confusion and possible lawsuits, we changed our name to TW4, which stood for *There Were Four*.

Socially during high school, when I wasn't practicing or playing gigs, I hung out with a small group of friends. Though we were all rather obviously gay—at least it was obvious to me—it was never something that we discussed. Rather, it was an unspoken bond that none of us were ready or willing to admit or say out loud. Our environment and Catholic upbringing did a very good job at repressing our sexuality—gay or straight. The human body was almost given a negative connotation—something that you should hide. We had a few sports teams and no physical-education classes. There was no such thing as sex education in health class—or any health class for that matter. We had strict dress codes that were designed to cover as much of the body as possible. If the sexual revolution was happening in other parts of the country, it was not flourishing at our little Chicago high school.

But somehow, our gang found each other. One boy, Michael, went on to become one of my lifelong friends. Another boy was very effeminate and was simply tortured by the other kids. Some other boys sang in the chorus, and another boy was in all the plays. None of us played on the sports teams. We all had our own outside interests that kept us busy, but girls weren't one of them.

It was apparent that none of us were clicking with the opposite sex like the straight boys were. We didn't sit around talking about cheerleaders' breasts, or how far we got with so-and-so last night. In that sense, our conversations were different than the typical high school boy's. Not that we discussed anything too personal. We were all still afraid of our feelings and certainly didn't know how to express them. Our conversations never got deeper than topics like music and movies and television shows. But nonetheless we found comfort in being together and found a sense of acceptance in each other's company.

A few of my buddies were interested in going out with girls. Not, of course, in the true sense, but at least to participate in the social aspects of dating. In order to be a part of the group, I remember making a few feeble attempts of my own at dating the opposite sex. For instance, one time I took my cousin to a school bonfire. Now that was awkward. Girls liked me, but if it got to a point where I thought one might like me too much, I backed away. I didn't want to have to explain it. And I thought, what's the point?

My friends and I hung around with one group of girls in particular. They were generally the "bad" girls of their school—a group of free-spirited party girls who liked to drink and have a good time, and perhaps for that reason couldn't find boyfriends of their own. So they adopted us instead. I believe this was long before the term "fag hag" became a staple of gay lingo. I don't particularly like the phrase, but it's used to refer to women who spend a lot of time with gay men. Our little group of girls and gay teenage boys may have been more ahead of the times than we knew.

When it came time for our senior prom, all of my buddies decided to go with these girls and some of their friends. They singled out one girl for me and asked if I would go with her. I can't say that I had a strong desire to go to the prom, but eventually I bent to peer pressure. I agreed to be her date. After all, it was the prom. It seemed like a rite of passage that you just couldn't miss. It's funny because John, who was clearly as heterosexual as they come, couldn't have cared less about the prom. In his opinion, he had no time for such silliness.

When the day came, I got all dressed up in my tuxedo. My mother took my picture and John snickered from the sidelines. Then I went off to pick up a date that I hardly knew. The girl and I had met once and spoke on the phone a few times to figure out the logistics of the evening. That was it. She was an Irish girl from a traditional Irish-Catholic family. When I went to pick her up at her house, it was like a scene from Peter Pan. As I stood in the living room waiting for her to come down the stairs, about twelve different ragamuffin heads popped up from various places in the room to check me out. A little head popped up from behind the couch, another little face from between the railing on the stairs. It was wild.

At the prom itself, I had an OK time. It was a typical 1960s prom—more like a school function than a date. The festivities were heavily monitored by chaperones who watched everything from what the girls wore—no exposed shoulders—to how close we were dancing. Even during the prom itself, I kept thinking, "Is this all there is? Is this the big deal about the prom?"

I became convinced that John probably had the right idea when he decided to stay at home. At the end of the night, I drove my date back to her house and walked her to the doorstep. I reached in—I'm not sure why—to try to give her a polite kiss goodnight. She turned her head before I could kiss her.

She said coolly, "Good night, Chuck. Thank you for taking me."

I said, "Sure. No problem." As she ducked back into Never Never Land, I thought, "She used me just like I used her. She needed a date to the prom."

What irony—if only she knew that I had more interest in kissing her older brother than in kissing her maybe she would have been less uptight.

————————

At our school, it was tradition that the day after the prom, all the kids met up at the beach. So the next day, my buddies and I all drove out to Indiana Dunes on Lake Michigan. Whereas the prom was a heavily orchestrated affair, the picnic at the beach was much looser. Everyone would bring some food and lots of beer. It was a time to party. And whereas the prior evening all the girls had been forced to keep their modesty in tact through a series of strict dress codes, today all rules were off. It was a hot June day and the girls dressed the part in the short shorts that were becoming popular and bikini tops. The mix of flimsy clothing and alcohol conspired to give the day an entirely different vibe than the night before.

My prom date and I managed to stay clear of each other give or take a smile and an averted glance every now and then. After all, the prom was over, so there was really no need for the niceties anymore. And besides, I was probably still a little pissed from the slight at the door the night before. There was, however, another girl who I was having a considerably harder time shaking off. She was one of the more popular girls—a high school "A-lister" to my "C-lister" status. Wherever I was that day, she seemed to be close by. I caught her staring at me a few times, and she seemed to be whispering about me with her friends. At first I thought it was my imagination—after all what would this girl want with me? She could have any boy there. But eventually one of her friends approached me.

"Margaret wants to see you down by the water," she said.

I was honestly confused. "Why?" I asked.

She kind of smiled in an odd way and said, "Why don't you go down and find out?"

I didn't want to be rude, so I slowly made my way down to the water where Margaret was sitting on some rocks all by herself. I said, "Hi. Your friend said you were looking for me."

She smiled, and motioned for me to come sit next to her. I joined her on the rocks. There was an awkward silence, and I was beginning to get the idea that Margaret didn't really have all that much to say to me. Maybe she had something else on her mind? I started talking nervously. "So, did you have a good time at the prom last night?"

She shrugged, "It was OK." Then she looked back at the crowd in the distance. "You here with a date?" she asked.

I said, "No, not really."

She said, "Good."

With that, it was only a minute before her lips reached up to mine. Before I knew exactly what was going on, we were kissing. I didn't hate it. It felt more like an out-of-body experience. Here I was kissing a girl I barely knew—a popular, good-looking girl who was most likely more than a little drunk—and all I could think about was how to get myself out of this situation without being a total jerk. If there was ever any question that this whole heterosexual thing wasn't going to work out for me—this took away all doubt.

After about a minute, I pulled away.

"I'm going to go back up with the group."

She looked shocked. I honestly don't think this girl had ever had something like this happen to her before. She said, "Why?"

I was honest. I simply said, "I'm just not into it. Sorry."

I felt bad for a day or two, wondering if I had hurt her feelings. But I'm fairly sure that, even though I'm telling this story years later, she probably forgot about the whole thing as quickly as she found her next conquest. For me, it was the first time that I was put in a situation with the opposite sex where something was expected of me. For her, I was just another boy at the beach. I'm sure she would be shocked to know the significance that our little kiss on the beach had in my life.

After graduation, the rest of the summer passed pretty much as expected. The band was keeping me busy playing parties, small clubs, dances, and fairs in the Chicago area. Of course, I was also busy planning the next stage of my life. My father was adamant that John and I go to college. As the son of a first-generation immigrant, my father had a dream of sending his children to college. In our neighborhood, very few of the men or women had college degrees. In my own family, even fewer. In fact, graduating from high school was actually an accomplishment. From the time I was quite young, I always knew that my parents were grooming me for college. They had sacrificed for years to make it happen. While Catholic schools were not expensive compared to today's private school tuitions, they did have yearly dues. It would have been less of a burden to send their children to public school—especially on a factory worker's salary—but my parents always found a way to come up with the extra money to send their kids to the "better" schools.

By now, however, TW4 was becoming so successful that I debated whether or not I really needed a bachelor's degree. I was already earning a steady income through music and I was only eighteen years old. I remember broaching the subject with my father.

"Dad," I said, "I was thinking. I'm making pretty good money with the band. Maybe I'll do this for a while and see what happens. College is expensive, and I could always go back if I change my mind."

My father wasn't the kind of man to raise his voice very often and in this case he didn't need to. Sometimes, when you see a certain look of disappointment in your parents' eyes, it's worth all the words in the world.

In the end, I decided to go to college. And it wasn't only my father's wish. It was mine too. At eighteen, I wasn't ready yet to give up on all my other options and pursue a career with the band fulltime. Even at this age, I realized that the possibility of TW4 "making it" was a long shot. Especially given our circumstances and where we lived, going to college to have something "to fall back on" seemed like the smartest option. We weren't growing up in Los Angeles or Motown—this was Roseland.

Other than music, the one other career that I could see myself in was teaching. Teaching was a profession that had always interested me. Throughout my parochial school education I had seen teachers use physical abuse and intimidation as a normal part of the teaching process. I believed—and still do—that the way to instill self-esteem in children isn't to knock them down in their early years, but rather to help them embrace their uniqueness. I knew there was a better way and I wanted to try to do things differently. So, I enrolled in a teaching college along with John. The school was known for years as the Chicago Teachers College, but subsequently changed its name to Chicago State College during my attendance. Dennis, who was about to go into his junior year, was already a student there. I majored in art—another lifelong interest—and John, like Dennis, majored in music.

During college I was dividing all of my time and energy between school and the band, conveniently ignoring my personal life. While I was becoming more cognizant of my sexuality, I still didn't know how to act on it. Programmed from a young age to believe that sex outside of marriage—even straight sex—was wrong, I was too immature to want or to enjoy sex. By age twenty, I had never gone out on a date or had any kind of sexual experience with a boy.

I think it's normal to start having experiences when you go to college. But my parents were very aware of the "free love" and drug culture that was springing up on college campuses, so they never let me or John go away on Spring Break or stay out all night. Neither of us was very rebellious when it came to our parents, so we stuck to their rules. And since Teachers College was a commuter school, I didn't have much opportunity to hang out partying in other students' dorm rooms, or to have the all-night talk sessions that are so much a part of most people's college experiences.

Outside of classes, the one activity that I did participate in was chorus. Our college actually had very strong choral group, and I remember being a little nervous trying out. But I did fine. In fact, I remember auditioning with one poor girl who didn't have a very good voice. The chorus instructor said to her in front of everyone, "I'm sorry, dear. You know you really should sing more like Charles."

I remember shrinking down in my seat thinking, "Oh no, did he really have to bring my name into this?" as the girl shrunk away.

John and Dennis were also part of the chorus. For us, and for many of the other students, this was our form of a fraternity. We didn't belong to any of the organized Greek houses. I couldn't really imagine myself hanging out with the frat boys. So instead, we hung out with the other students in the chorus at practices and around campus.

Every day before classes or during breaks, the students would congregate in the student center's cafeteria. Since there were quite a few music majors at our school, and since this was also the era of the folk singer, it was inevitable that three or four students would start singing together around one of the tables. It was not uncommon to find John or Dennis or me joining in. We were already quite well known as the "guys in the band," since we would frequently play at fraternity and sorority parties around campus. The other students would always give us a great reception whenever we played, so these impromptu jam sessions were just another way to perform for our growing fan base around campus.

Of course, we weren't the only ones performing in the cafeteria. There were many talented students in our school, and all were eager to be heard. It was a time of social unrest in the country, and music seemed to be a great way for young people to express themselves. There were quite a few budding Bob Dylans roaming campus. There were also quite a few talented black musicians at our school who used music as a way to constructively express their views of the world. By my last year of college, in 1969, race riots had begun to spring up on campus, which made it even nicer that all of us in chorus—black, white, and other—had found such a peaceful way to become friends and harmonize together.

One day, John, Dennis, and I were in the cafeteria together when we saw another student named John Curulewski playing guitar. We were all impressed at how well he played. As fate would have it, Tom had recently left TW4, so we were looking for a new guitar player. It didn't take long for us to agree—John C. would be the perfect replacement. Dennis approached him, and invited him to join our band. Fortunately, John C. was familiar with the band from seeing us play around the school, and he accepted our offer. TW4 survived our first experience of having to replace a member of the band. It certainly wouldn't be our last. John was a great addition, and his solid guitar playing made our band even stronger.

I followed the same general routine for all four years during college. I would go to class, go home, do my school work, rehearse, and play gigs. That took up all of my free time. As a result, my personal life didn't progress very far; I convinced myself that academics and the band were more important. I just didn't have time for a personal life.

Of course, this was an excuse for not having the courage to face my feelings. It was one thing to know what I was feeling toward men, but if I didn't act on it, it wasn't anything that I had to deal with. It wasn't as real. Maybe I'm rationalizing, but sometimes I think it was for the best that I didn't have sex while I was still in college. I'm only half joking when I say that I might never have graduated. I don't know that I would have been mature enough to handle it. I could see myself saying, "Woo hoo, this is great," and totally get out of control.

This isn't to say that I wasn't becoming increasingly curious. I knew that there were other gay men out there, and now that I was an adult, it was becoming harder to suppress my interest in this life. My first attempt at exploration began when I was about twenty years old when I was a sophomore. There was a newspaper in town that used to advertise a theater that showed gay pornography. I must have looked at that advertisement a hundred times, picking up the paper then setting it back down. Each week that the paper came out, I would buy a copy and look for the ad. I memorized the address. I plotted out how far it was from my home and school, and calculated the chances of someone I knew seeing me going in. One day, I finally mustered up the courage to go there. I wanted to see what it was all about.

The movie theater was in Old Town, outside of my neighborhood, so I was fairly confident that I could slip in without seeing anyone who might know me, or vice versa. Still a virgin, I had no idea what to expect. I was not acquainted at all with the intricacies of gay sex. In all, honesty, I was frightened to death. Only the darkness of the theater gave me the courage that I needed to actually buy a ticket and step inside the door.

Once inside the dingy, dirty theatre, I found myself surrounded by other gay men of all ages for the first time in my life. I didn't know how to react, and I wasn't even sure if I belonged there. I slumped down in the seat looking straight ahead, thinking, "What the hell am I doing here?" But it was also exciting. I was about to get a peek into a world that I had only imagined. Curiosity kept me from leaving.

When the movie began, I looked up at the screen, and as the larger than life images flickered across the half-empty theater. I said, "OK, I get it. That's what's going on out there."

I wasn't quite sure that I was ready to participate in these particular acts, but at least these skin flicks validated the fact that there were other people out there like me. I wasn't alone. I had been living in an isolated world, but suddenly everything made more sense. When one of the guys in the theatre sat next to me and put his hand on my thigh, I stood up and left.

This foray into the gay world was short-lived. After my initial visit to the theatre, I didn't go back for a long time. I didn't need any more for now. Finally, I felt validated and I knew that when I was ready, there was a life outside my sheltered world where I would be understood and fulfilled. But I wasn't ready for that yet. For one thing, I didn't want to do anything that might shift my focus from the band, which had become the most fulfilling part of my life. It was such convenient diversion.

By the time I was in my senior year of college, TW4 was becoming one of the hottest cover bands in Chicago. The other musicians in the Chicago music scene at the time couldn't figure it out. Quite honestly, I couldn't either. The musical landscape was changing. The early Beatles had dominated the music scene in the mid-1960s. But Woodstock in 1969 had changed everything, and the early Beatles sound was slowly being pushed out by the hippie generation's more drug-hazed rock. That was a difficult transition for us to make. We weren't dropping acid. We didn't have the longhaired hippie look. Our music was still much more influenced by the Beatles than by the Doors.

Here we were—clean cut, college educated, and well dressed. We weren't the typical rock band anymore. But somehow, our little basement trio was taking gigs away from the stud rockers who were competing for the same jobs. In my head, this was even more reason to keep the issue of my sexual orientation far in the background. I didn't want to make waves—and I certainly didn't want to give anyone more of a reason to question our place on the rock-music scene.

The more popular we became, the more I began to wonder what would happen if anyone found out that I was gay. Would that be the end of it? This made me even more reluctant to begin exploring my sexuality. Playing in the hottest band around was a sort of redemption from the barbs and abuse that had haunted me in the early part of my school life. I wasn't going to mess around with that. After all, it was only the late 1960s. Even in 2006, a popular musician will sometimes feel the need to hide the fact that he or she is gay. I didn't want to risk being found out. Today, you see guys like Lance Bass—a poster child for one of the most popular teen heartthrob bands in history—coming out on the cover of *People* magazine. Back then, you couldn't name one gay musician.

After my visit to the movie theater, though, I had opened up a part of myself that I would never again be able to ignore completely. Keeping my secret was becoming more of a challenge than it ever had been before. I wasn't a child anymore. A part of me—the adult part—resented having to hide my identity from everyone I cared about. Eventually, something inside of me snapped. I just couldn't take it anymore. I needed to tell someone. I needed to say it out loud, "I'm gay," if just once.

So, of course, I turned to John, the one person in the world I trusted above all others. From our days back on the playground, I knew that John would always be protective of me—no matter what. Up until that point, if he suspected that I was gay, he never mentioned it to me. Now, I was about to test his limits of unconditional love.

We were riding in the car. John and his future wife, Debbie, were sitting in the front, and I was riding in the backseat. I liked Debbie very much at the time; she was a sweet girl. In fact, I always used to tell her she was too good for my brother. Something inside of me said, "Now is the time. Just say it."

I took a deep breath, and started speaking before my brain could figure out what was happening, "Hey, guys," I said. "I want to tell you something." I got their attention. "I want you to know something. I'm gay."

There was silence. We rode along looking straight ahead. I started to wonder if I had made a mistake.

"It's no big deal. I just wanted you know."

Then John spoke, "So that's why you acted the way you did when you were a kid."

I said, "Gee, thanks, John," heavy on the sarcasm.

Then Debbie said what my brother could not. She looked back and said, "It doesn't matter, Chuck. We still love you."

I said, "Thanks, Debbie." And with that there was nothing more any of us needed to say.

Shortly after I told my brother and sister-in-law, I knew that I needed to tell one more person. I called my sister on the phone. I said, "Emily, I told John and Debbie, and want you to know too. I'm gay."

She didn't miss a beat, before she responded, "Oh Chuck. I'm sure you're just going through a phase." I knew she really didn't want me to argue, so I said, "Maybe, Emily. Maybe . . ."

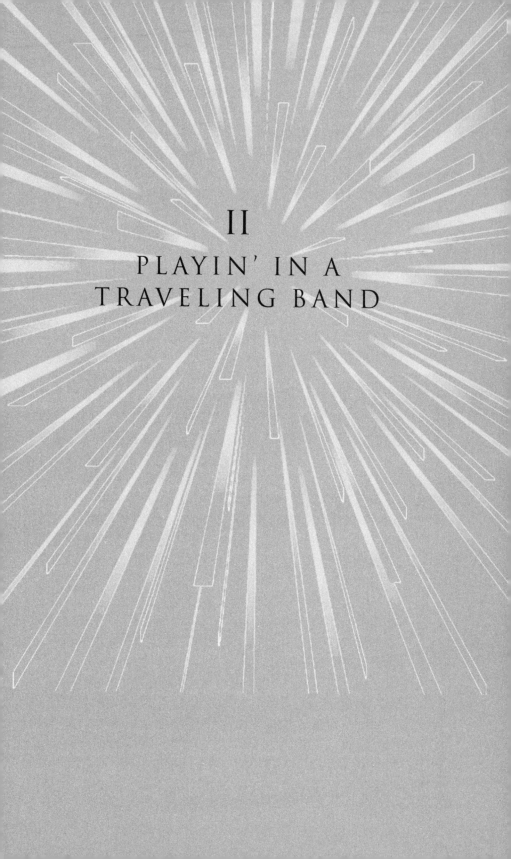

II
PLAYIN' IN A
TRAVELING BAND

CHAPTER FIVE

THE WOODEN
NICKEL YEARS

In many ways, 1970 was an important year. First of all, I graduated from college and became a teacher. This made my parents extremely proud. I remember graduation day. After the ceremony, I said to my father, "I may have earned the degree, but this belongs to you." And it was true. Without my parents' support and encouragement, I never would have made it to college.

I had majored in art, which matched my lifelong interest in colors and visuals with my desire to help children grow and learn. After graduating in December, I was a student-teacher for a semester, then was lucky enough to get a full-time teaching assignment at Christian Fenger High School. It was only about ten minutes away from my house, and it was actually the high school that my mother had attended.

At one point, Fenger was one of the best schools in the area. But the neighborhood and the times were changing. When I got my teaching assignment the student body was composed mostly of underprivileged students. By the time these kids got to high school, they already had a lot of baggage with them. Drugs were very prevalent at the time, yet there were no drug prevention programs to help steer them away from making the wrong choices. Teen pregnancy was also a big problem. Yet, again, there were no sex education programs to help these young boys and girls understand the ramifications of their behavior.

Most of these girls got pregnant because they simply weren't given enough information to prevent it. The world treated them like thirty-five-year-old women, but they were just girls. They may have looked older, but they were kids.

Seeing all this was a bit disheartening. It was a hard environment to teach in—a hard environment to try to make a difference. That this was the first time I had a class of my own didn't make matters any easier. I remember the first day that I walked into the classroom. Some of these kids looked like they were about two years younger and two feet taller than I was. Great! But once I started interacting with the class, it was less intimidating. They may have looked threatening, but they were just kids. I tried to show them respect, and for the most part, they responded. When I did have to discipline any of the boys and they would complain, I would say, "You want to be treated like a man, start acting like one." I think they respected my attitude.

I was also one of the few male art teachers at the school, and of course I was very young. Both of these factors prompted the other female art teachers to treat me like a cub scout. They were very supportive and gave me tips on how to keep the kids under control. Looking back, they probably felt sorry for me. I was not much older than the students, and they probably thought that I was going to be eaten alive. So, the other teachers looked out for me, and guided me, and seemed generally amused to have me around the school.

Their support really helped. I enjoyed teaching and I tried to create a passion in the kids. And the truth is, I think I was pretty good at it. But teaching is difficult, particularly at an inner-city school. Very often I felt like I was babysitting rather than teaching a class in art. During that year of teaching, I knew that if I decided to continue on that career path, I would want to get a higher degree and teach at a higher level. I give teachers tremendous credit—it's not an easy job.

My other bandmates were also teaching at the time. John got his degree in music and taught band, and Dennis went on to teach music theory. I think this fact would probably amuse die-hard rock fans. That's what made us so different. Can you see walking into a classroom and having Gene Simmons or Ozzy Osbourne as your homeroom teacher? It's a funny concept. So, by day, we were mild-mannered teachers, and at night, we were musicians with fans our students' age who would come and scream for us on stage. Putting myself in the reverse position, I just can't imagine it. When I was in high school, I thought all my teachers were ancient—and certainly not cool. Maybe my kids thought the same about me—but that was probably for the best. I really didn't want them to know about my other life. Luckily, I was good at keeping all kinds of secrets.

We worked all the time. In addition to our day jobs Monday through Friday, we were spending weekends playing music. By now, we had moved beyond playing the *Animal House*–type frat parties that were a staple of our music schedule during college. Now, we made our money by playing proms, weddings, or more upscale social gatherings. At the time, we were still doing mostly covers. We could take any song right off of the radio, listen to it a few times, figure out the riffs, and make it sound great. That's what the wedding crowds wanted to hear. It paid the bills. But while we were a wedding band, we also strove to be something more. We wanted to introduce some original music. We didn't want to just be a band that you could dance to; we wanted to be band that you could listen to.

This brings me to the other important thing that happened in 1970. Despite our acronym TW4 (which stood for "There Were 4") our band actually grew to five that year with the addition of James "JY" Young. To perform rock music the way it was meant to sound, we needed a strong lead guitarist, and JY was one of the best in the area. He had been playing with a band that did totally different music than we did. His musical tastes veered more toward heavy metal and Jimi Hendrix, which wasn't our style. JY even looked a little different than the rest of us. Very tall, with long, straight blond hair, he was an imposing figure on stage. Despite these seeming contradictions, however, JY knew that TW4 was a top cover band. Also playing in our favor was the fact that the band he had been playing with broke up after one of its members decided to become a Jehovah's Witness. He was available. So, JY agreed to join our group.

I don't know if he was entirely sold on our sound at the time—we were becoming more influenced by the British bands—Yes; Emerson, Lake & Palmer; Genesis—than the acid rock that James was used to playing. But we were getting a lot of work, and JY needed a job. So, he wholeheartedly came on board. Despite our musical differences, JY's style turned out to be a great complement to TW4. He made our sound stronger—more authentic and more complex.

TW4 was becoming the envy of all the bands on the South Side because we were getting all the jobs. No matter how hard the other guys tried, our five-man band was the crowd pleaser. So, despite our ongoing success working parties and weddings, we knew it was time to start branching out. We wanted to start getting into rock 'n' roll show-cases, which was the only way a serious band could make a name for itself and start playing original music. Of course, breaking into this world wasn't easy. Just like today, it often means playing in small music clubs for little or no money just to get a foot in the door. Since we didn't fit the standard acid rocker look of the day, it was even harder for us to break into this world. Generally, we weren't what the club owners were expecting.

But slowly, we started making inroads. For a while, we played the bars on Rush Street—a popular street in Chicago filled with bars and restaurants. Primarily, you went to Rush Street on the weekends to drink, meet members of the opposite sex, and party. You did not go to appreciate the music. It was a meat market. I suppose if a musician was into that scene, it could have been a decent area to play. You could definitely get some action. And in truth, many local bands were clearly just out to have a good time before they hung it all up to go become accountants. But we had higher aspirations, and none of us enjoyed this environment. Most of the guys in the group had girlfriends or wives. I was gay. So for us, playing these clubs got to be a bit humiliating.

Looking out from a small stage, seeing people talking and screaming and getting drunk while you are playing your heart out is not a good thing. You become background music. I know it can be par for the course, and I feel bad for bands that get stuck in the rut of playing for audiences who could really care less about hearing their music. We decided, however, that this wasn't for us, that we wouldn't play these kinds of dances and more.

We searched out the more serious music venues. In the beginning, one of our favorite places to play was a tiny neighborhood joint called the Knotty Pine. We made no money, but it gave us a chance to hone our music and gain confidence. We used to attract a crowd there whenever we played. Usually it was filled with a fair amount of friends and relatives and people from the neighborhood who knew us forever. The Knotty Pine was really important to us in the early part of our career. It can get really tough out there trying to make a name in the music scene. It can rattle your faith in your ability and shake your confidence. But playing at the Knotty Pine, where we had so much support and encouragement for our music, gave us the confidence to keep plugging away. Moreover, we were building a core fan base that was starting to follow us to other parts of the city.

This experience gave us the confidence to venture outside of our comfort zone. On the North Side of Chicago, there was another very popular and well-respected music club called Alice's Revisited. It was right next to the El track in a funky part of town. All the "serious" rock groups, and even jazz and blues groups, played Alice's. They didn't serve alcohol, so everyone there was actually interested in listening to the music. Eventually, bolstered by our Knotty Pine success, we decided to give it a try. We got a gig in the most unappealing, earliest time slot that they could give us. I remember walking into the place and getting looks from the management like, "What are you guys doing here?" Outside of JY, who sported long blond hair, we didn't have the look of the usual musicians, or most of the patrons. But, we did our thing.

The first time that we played at Alice's Revisited, we had about ten people come to watch us. Amazingly, we were invited back. The second week that we played, we had about 100 people turn out. And the third week, we had 500 people in the audience. Obviously, we were doing something right.

By playing these kinds of music clubs and getting our name out, we eventually attracted the attention of some local music promoters who ran rock 'n' roll shows. These were the people who really understood what we were doing. Once we got involved with the promoters, playing the dances and weddings started to become more and more unbearable. By our own doing, the wedding dates started to dry up. We began to get into our own original songs and playing covers that were for the most part undanceable.

When I was a kid, I used to hear commercials for the "Wild Goose" concerts hosted by Dex Card—a radio disc jockey on WLS. Back then, I remember thinking, "Boy, if only we could play the Dex Card Wild Goose Club—we'd have it made." Well, eventually my wish came true. One day, Dex Card called. Dex was an extremely well-connected radio disc jockey and concert promoter in the Chicago area. All week on his radio show, he would announce that "such and such bands" would be playing at a particular venue the coming weekend. These Dex Card "Wild Goose" concerts would draw teenagers and young people who would drive miles to the given destination each week to hear their favorite bands. Many of the concerts were held in Indiana, but they also had them in Oak Park and other areas around the city.

By playing these Wild Goose concerts, we gained exposure across the entire Greater Chicago area. Dex came to love us and I know why; we were making him a ton of cash. TW4 consistently broke attendance records for the venues that we played. As a band, we were tireless. We had to be. You were only as good as your last ticket sale. Basically, the way it worked was that your manager—at the time another neighborhood friend named Vince—would get you an audition with a pro-moter. If the promoter liked you, you would get one shot. If the crowd liked you, the promoter invited you back. If not, you were out.

We never wanted to blow our one shot, so we would give 100 percent every time we went out to play. And we would play everywhere we were invited. If the place had an amp hook up and a crowd, we were there. This constant exposure helped to build our fan base. Even-tually, it paid off. TW4 got the attention of a local record label.

One night, Bill Traut, the president of Chicago-based Wooden Nickel Records—a local subsidiary of RCA—came to see us play at a club. The next day, he called our manager Vince and said that he would like to meet us to discuss a record deal. We said, "A record deal, are you kidding me?" Obviously, we jumped on it. The fact that a record company was interested in our group was extremely flattering. Someone got us.

Our manager told us that the president wanted to meet us in his office to discuss signing with his label. So we all got in the car and drove to the designated address. Now, you would normally expect a record company's offices to be in a huge office building with a roster of names on the door. Not this time. We pulled up to a condominium building and looked at each other bewilderedly. I remember saying, "Do you think this is it? Do we have the right address?" We walked up to door and found the guy's name on the residents' listing. He buzzed us up to his condo.

We knocked on the door. The five of us were hovering expectantly around his door, when we saw his head peek out. He may or may not have been wearing a bathrobe, but my memory says he was. He quickly ushered us into this "office," which was actually an office, living room, and bedroom combination. This guy did everything there. It was a little gross.

I immediately knew that this guy was quite a character. He was nice enough, but the most unexecutive executive I have ever met. There were other clues too that gave me cause for concern. Looking around the "office" I noticed one album by each of Wooden Nickel's signed artists. There were never two. Not a good sign. This label was clearly interested in finding talent, making a fast buck, and moving on. They didn't know a thing about career development and really didn't care.

When we got outside, I mentioned my concerns to the other guys. I think we all felt that this might not be the ideal situation. But at the time, we all wanted a record deal so badly that we overlooked the obvious. It was dangerous to ask too many questions. And at the time, there were no other big-time record labels banging down our door.

So, a few days later we proceeded to sign our lives away, then went out and celebrated. As I remember, we were each given a signing gift from the president too—a small token of his appreciation from the local drug paraphernalia shop. Granted, it wasn't Tiffany's, but we were so thrilled that we had finally gotten a record deal that nothing could have ruined the moment.

After all, we had spent the last few years playing every little joint that would ask us to perform just to be seen and heard. For a while, when we started seeing the longhaired hippie bands infiltrating the clubs, we thought we were dead in the water. But now, here we were with a record deal. In the end, we had skyrocketed past the hippie rockers, leaving them dumbstruck—long hair blowing in the wind!

The first thing that the record company made us do was change our name. TW4 was not going to cut it. They allowed us to choose our new name, which wasn't an easy task for five opinionated musicians. We must have gone through a hundred names. One of us would always find something wrong with whatever name the others would suggest. It was frustrating to go through all the haggling, but we needed a name. Finally, we decided to each write our favorite name on a piece of paper and throw them into a hat.

The only suggested name that no one in the band actively hated was Styx. We all got the reference to Greek mythology and thought, "Hey, that really means something." In mythology, Styx is the winding river in Hades, the underworld, which separates the world of the living from the world of the dead. That was kind of a cool concept for a rock band: "Listen to our music and cross over into another realm of existence." Or something like that. Besides, even if no one else got it, mystical sounding names were very seventies. So, Styx was born. Of course, at the beginning, everybody thought our name was Sticks, but eventually they got it.

Shortly after signing with Wooden Nickel, Styx went into the studio to begin recording our first album. Since we all had day jobs at the time, we could only record at night. This was not the multimillion-dollar record contract that you hear about these days, so the old adage, "Don't quit your day job," definitely applied. We got our recording deal while I was still in the first full year of teaching high school. After working all day with the kids, I would grab some food and drive over to the studio where we would rehearse and record the album. It was a grueling schedule for all of us, but we were young and excited, so the adrenaline carried us through our exhaustion.

Inside the recording studio, I started picking up on some of the same vibes that I got that first day in the president's condo. When John started setting up his equipment, he had a lot of different percussion instruments in addition to his drums. The producer saw them and basically told John that he was wasting his time with all that stuff. I couldn't believe that a professional record producer wouldn't appreciate the complexity that those instruments brought to our sound. But again, we wanted to cut a record, so we plowed ahead.

Our first album was released in 1972. It was called, for obvious reasons, *Styx*. Since Wooden Nickel rarely made two albums with any group, perhaps they didn't feel the need to be any more creative with the name. Its release coincided with the end of the school year. As a group, we all had a decision to make. If we were going to try to make this album go anywhere, we were going to have to go out on tour and promote it. If we were going out on tour, we couldn't keep our day jobs. It was time to decide just how committed we were to Styx. After a bit of deliberation, all of us agreed that we would go out to promote this album as a group. In the end, I really don't think any of us would have had it any other way.

Now the hard part: telling my parents that John and I were leaving our teaching jobs to go on the road. Needless to say, the news didn't go over well. While they had been happy about the record deal, I don't think my parents thought anything serious would ever come from our music. To them, it was a hobby. And it's understandable. In our neighborhood, people had sensible jobs. If you were lucky enough to go into a profession like teaching that did not involve working in factories or plants, you didn't walk away. And you certainly did not leave a steady teaching job for the dream of becoming a rock star.

John and I went to talk to my parents together. When John told them that he was leaving his teaching job to work full-time with the band, I'm sure they thought, "There goes John again, doing some other nutty thing like he usually does." Also, John was such a natural talent on the drums and I think they assumed he might go into music professionally one day, just like my Uncle Tony. For me, on the other hand, I was the stable one. For me, they saw a teacher. My parents told me once that during the Great Depression, teachers were the only ones with recession-proof jobs. They saw this career path as a guarantee of lifetime employment. So, when I told them that I was not returning to my teaching job either, they were shocked. My father was particularly disappointed.

"You go and do this—you'll end up a bum on the street," he told me.

I said, "No, dad. I might become a lot of things, but never a bum. If I don't do this now, it's going to go away. I'm twenty-three years old. I worked hard for this for ten years. If I don't walk through this door, it's going to close forever. If I don't take this chance, we'll always be a weekend cover band playing Bar Mitzvahs and lounges."

It was hard to go against my father. But, while I liked teaching and I loved working with the kids, the choice to leave was easy. To me, teaching was the hobby and music was my passion. I had gone to college partly to please my father, but this time I was choosing music for me. I had spent my life trying to make my folks happy—now it was time to make myself happy.

I know my father would have been amazed at, and very proud of, what actually transpired. All he ever wanted was a better life for his children than he had had for himself. That's why schooling was so important to him. He never had the chance to get a proper education. When he was one year old, his own father was killed in an industrial accident. This left his mother, my grandmother, a widow with two young children. She barely spoke English. She had no education. She had no means of supporting herself or her family. In desperation, she married again to an ogre of a man who was an alcoholic. She went on to have five more children with him.

When my father finished the eighth grade, he was forced to drop out of high school and take a job to help support his family. I always respected him so much for doing this rather than running away, especially since his home life under his stepfather was so tough. Sometimes, his stepfather would hit my grandmother in a drunken rage. My father, who was a short man, was the only one who would stand up to him. He loved his mother and always protected her from this horrible man. I think that shows a great deal of character.

During World War II, my father went into the service. After he was released, he had a very hard time getting work. He finally took a factory job at a steel plant in Gary, Indiana. Every day throughout my childhood, my father took a bus to a train and made the sixty-mile commute to the steel plant. John and I used to wait at the bus stop and walk him home. I remember how tired his face would look as he stepped off the bus. On the rare days that he drove to work, the car would be filled with about a quarter-inch of steel dust when he returned. It was not only brainless work; it was dangerous work. Eventually, the environmental conditions took their toll on my father's health.

I know that I am lucky to have escaped this kind of life myself. One summer during high school, I took a summer job at a local Sherwin-Williams plant. It was a huge plant that employed a large part of our community. When I first started working there, I remember opening up gigantic valves that would pour out benzene, a nasty, carcinogenic paint remover that we would use to clean up paint. It would splash all over. We weren't given any eye or body protection. We didn't even use rubber gloves when we mopped up the floors.

I had a friend who worked there too. We were like the Laverne and Shirley of the paint factory. We were always talking and laughing with each other. During one of our conversations, we realized that about 600 gallons of paint were overflowing onto the floor. I was sure we were going to get fired. But when we told the supervisor, he just told us to clean it up. After that incident, they separated us. The supervisor said, "I think you two make a better team apart."

I got sent to the dye department. It was called P.C. Blue. We baked it in hot ovens then scraped off the powder cakes. The dust would go into your pores, on your skin, and up your nose. When I would get home, I couldn't wash the blue off of my hands. When I sneezed, blue powder came out of my nose. It was disgusting.

I hated that job. My father would come into the room that I shared with John to wake me up in the morning. After he left, I remember pounding on my pillow, "I hate this job! I hate this job!" But I didn't want to disappoint my father, so I kept going. Even one of the old-time plant workers took me aside and tried to warn me. He said, "Chuck, I've been doing this job for a long time. You're a young man. After this summer I don't want to ever see you taking this job again, do you hear me?"

Finally, my brother and sister convinced my parents that they shouldn't let me go to the job anymore. They said, "There's blue stuff coming out of Chuck's nose. It's not right." My parents let me quit. A few years later, we were talking about working at the plant, and my aunt said, "I don't see the big deal. It was a good job." That was the mindset. As long as you were making money, you just put up with the other stuff, even if it was going to kill you.

Shortly after we went on the road to begin promoting our first album, dad started feeling ill. He went to one doctor who told him that it was nothing. Dad went back to work. But his stomach problems wouldn't go away. We got a second opinion. A few days later, the doctor called my mother and me into his office to deliver the test results. In those days, when there was bad news, doctors would often tell the patient's family rather than telling the patient directly. I never understood this. It was as if by not talking about it, it would somehow go away. I suppose the thinking was that somehow it protected the patient, but I think it's worse if the patient can't prepare himself for what's going on. I had many arguments with my mother over this, but in the end I had to respect her wishes. Dad would be spared as many details as possible throughout his illness.

The second doctor saw a tumor on my father's stomach that was likely cancerous. He had to have surgery. My father went into the hospital to have the tumor removed. After the operation, the doctor came out to see the family. My mother, brother, sister, and I were all there. The doctor said that the tumor was worse than they had originally thought. He had removed my father's stomach and pancreas, creating a makeshift stomach out of my father's intestine. He told us that the cancer was now generalized throughout his entire body. We all started crying together. I knew I wasn't going to have my father much longer.

For the next eight months, my dad remained in the hospital. He received chemotherapy, which made him feel even sicker, but there was really nothing that they could do to help him. Every day during his hospital stay, I would go to the hospital with my mother to see him. My sister and brother, who were each married by this time, assumed that I would handle the brunt of the responsibility. And honestly, I didn't mind. I wanted to spend this time with my father. During those eight months, I feel I bonded with my father more strongly than ever before.

On New Year's Eve that year, I was invited to a party.

I said, "No, I can't go. My father is going to die soon."

Two days later, he passed away. At first I was angry. He was still a young man, and I felt robbed. I was angry with God. In time, however,

I realized that we all have our time to go. I could miss my father—I still do to this day. I could grieve for my father. But I was doing nobody any good by getting angry. Eventually, I let the anger go.

I have no guilt. I did everything that I could during the last days of his life to show him how much I loved him. My only regret is that he never had the opportunity to see his sons achieve success with our music. He may have passed away worrying that the two of us would end up destitute old men. I think he would have gotten a kick out of what actually happened. I think he would have been proud.

At the time of my father's death, we were just beginning our journey. Unbelievably, despite a fairly lackluster promotional effort by the record company for the *Styx* album, one of the singles from the record actually became a hit.

The song "Best Thing," written by JY and Dennis, debuted on the charts at #88. We were thrilled and couldn't wait to watch its meteoric climb up the charts. The second week it reached #82. Excellent. By the third week . . . "What? I don't see it!" Yes, it was off the charts. Ok, so we learned a lesson. Maybe this was going to take a little longer than expected.

Nonetheless, we got a taste of success, and it was addictive. "Best Thing," was the first Styx song that I ever heard played on the radio. It's an amazing feeling to hear one of your songs played on the air. Even today, every time I hear a Styx song, it's a rush. My mind always goes back to a rehearsal, or to laying the track, or to some other aspect of recording the song.

The record was successful enough that the record company wanted us to crank out our next album as quickly as possible. After "Best Thing" hit the charts, we felt good about our future. So in 1973, when we recorded our second album, *Styx II*, we had high hopes for it. But, true to its track record, Wooden Nickel spent almost nothing on promotions. In fact, we later found out that they spent some $160-odd dollars on marketing—all on postage stamps to mail the record to radio stations. That was it. If some program director in Topeka opened the package without throwing it in the waste can, great. If not, we were out of luck. We also had very little distribution in record stores. So, even if one of our songs actually got played on the air and somebody liked it enough to buy it—they couldn't. If you didn't have retail distribution, there was no way for anyone to buy your album. Ironically, forty years later, you can buy more songs from *Styx II* now, via the Internet, than you could at the time of its release.

On the second album, Dennis wrote quite a few of the songs himself, including the song "Lady," Dennis's passionate love song dedicated to his wife Suzanne. Despite the limited promotion of the album, "Lady" did manage to find its way onto a few radio stations across the country. For one thing, we sang it live at all of our concerts, which got the attention of some program directors in the areas where we toured. Fan reaction to the song was always strong, and we had a hunch that it might be a hit if only more people could hear it—or buy it.

At that point, we all realized that if Styx was going to make it, we were going to have to get out there and make it happen ourselves. The record company wasn't going to do it for us. Once you get a record deal, people think, "Wow, you've made it." But actually, once you get a record deal, that's when the games begin. All of a sudden, you have to prove yourself and start making money for your record company. If you blow your first shot at a recording deal, there might never be another one. Another record company would be reluctant to sign a group that already lost money on an album. And even though we were being set up for failure in a sense, record executives aren't interested in excuses. So, we began to take matters into our hands.

Two years after we released our first album, we got the break that changed the course of our career. In 1974, after releasing our fourth album for Wooden Nickel called *Man of Miracles*, we visited radio station WLS in Chicago to try to convince them to play something off of our new album. In those days, radio was much less corporate, and it wasn't uncommon for bands to visit stations and try to get in good with everyone from the receptionist to the program director. You could do this anyway that worked—from sending flowers to the receptionist, to indulging the program directors with gifts or their favorite recreational substances—it was the 1970s after all. Major market radio stations had tremendous power to make or break careers. Program directors, even disc jockeys themselves, had the power to make decisions independently based on instinct and their own personal likes and dislikes. Music wasn't focus-grouped to death in those days, which helped create energy on the best radio stations.

Unfortunately, nobody at WLS was interested in playing anything off of Man of Miracles. They turned us down with a "Thanks, but no thanks." But the program director had a surprise in store for us. He said that while he wasn't going to play our new stuff, he was interested in one of our older cuts. It turned out that he was still getting requests from fans to play our song "Lady," which had been released almost two years earlier on our Styx II album. He said that he thought it was a hit song that nobody had ever gotten behind, and he wanted to change things. The program director announced that he was going to play the song every night at 8 p.m. until it was a hit. It worked.

At the time, WLS was one of the most influential radio stations in the country. It was a powerful clear-channel AM rock station that could be heard across several states at night. Its support of "Lady" started a groundswell that eventually got the attention of RCA, Wooden Nickel's parent company. Wooden Nickel re-released the song, this time with promotional support from RCA. That was all it took. "Lady" hit #6 on the Billboard charts and we had our first gold record. Slowly, with RCA's support, "Lady" began to make the charts city by city across the country and was often the #1 played song in any given market.

"Lady" put the name Styx on the map. However, after the initial groundswell of fame that the song brought, the band went back into a bit of a slump. Man of Miracles—our last album with Wooden Nickel—didn't really take off. One song, "You Need Love," charted at #88 and never rose any higher. It was a disappointment. But we didn't slow down. If anything, after the success of "Lady" the band got busier than ever.

Styx was with Wooden Nickel for four years. During that time, we toured almost constantly. We piled our instruments and ourselves into our cars, or trucks or whatever we were driving at the time, and hit every local music venue in the greater Illinois region. In the beginning, we played primarily in the Chicago area. With our roots in the South Side, even playing on the North Side was a big deal.

But we didn't want to stay a regional band. So we started branching out to neighboring states like Indiana and Wisconsin. We were popular with promoters because we always did a great job and we had a big following. A lot of our fan base grew from word-of-mouth, grassroots marketing. There was no such thing as MTV back then, so short of playing something like the *Ed Sullivan Show* or *American Bandstand*, there was really no way to gain national exposure without paying some dues.

Eventually, our manager Vince started getting us dates in cities all over the United States. We started playing states as far away as Pennsylvania and West Virginia to the east, and Utah to the west. This is when things got really interesting. We still didn't fly. The record company wasn't giving us any travel dollars and we couldn't afford the airfare for five guys, plus equipment. So we continued to rent station wagons and vans and took turns driving across America. I remember driving through the Smoky Mountains, sitting backward in one of those pull-up seats that face the rear window, with no idea where the hell we were going because all I could see were the backs of the road signs. I saw a lot of little towns that way across Alabama, Mississippi, and Texas.

Once we got to our destination, we would pack into the nearest Holiday Inn, or the cheapest place we could find, usually bunking two in a room. We would survive on pizza, fast food, and beer. When it came time to actually play, we would drive to the venue, haul out our equipment, and set it up ourselves. After our set, we would break it down, load it back up, and start the whole process over again the next day.

It was a hard life. Every penny that we made, we put back into the business. None of us had any money. I got used to skipping meals on the road, and I still lived at home when we were back in Chicago. I suppose in some ways it was easier for me; life on the road with no money was particularly hard on the guys who were married. Dennis even had a child to support. It got frustrating at times, especially as we put out each album. You couldn't help thinking, "We made four albums. So this is the big time?"

Something inside kept us going. We all believed that if we just got out there on the grassroots level, someday it would all pay off. Of course, when I'm philosophical about it all, I believe it happened for a reason. Traveling and performing so much, under such Spartan conditions, built character and made us better performers. It was a great training ground for things to come; serving as the novices before becoming the craftsmen. Sometimes I look at shows like *American Idol* and wonder if those kids are really going to be ready for what's about to happen to them. We were never given the luxury of finding out what instant success is like. But despite the forces pulling us away from our dream, we never gave up. We kept our focus and supported each other. I'm proud of that even today.

We were on the road for weeks at a time. When I think back, I can't believe we worked that hard. But when you're in it, you don't realize. There were some fun times too. We were all in our early twenties and typical young goofballs. When we would finish playing at night and got back to our hotel rooms, the adrenaline rush from performing would be still be going strong. Wrestling matches would often break out, with John tackling JY or me to the ground. We'd stay up for hours, eating and having a few drinks to relax.

Being typical brothers, sometimes on the road the relationship between John and me would slip into the juvenile territory that happens between siblings. We were buddies, but we had our share of fights.

I remember one particular argument where we tried to kick the shit out of each other while driving, with John in the front seat and me in the back, and the rest of the band taking cover in between.

Despite spending so much time together, or perhaps because of it, the band didn't do all that much socializing outside of work. The other guys all had personal lives outside of the band. Dennis had a girlfriend from high school who eventually became his wife, Suzanne. John married Debbie. JY also had a girlfriend, Susie, whom he later married. On the road, we basically drove, performed, and slept. When we were back home in Chicago, on the weekends we played our gigs, then went our separate ways. Outside of the band, I really had very little in common with the other guys. And honestly, they had little in common with me, except the idea of music. In other words, we weren't The Monkees.

I suppose this separation between our professional and personal lives made it easier to keep my secret. My brother John was still the only band member who I ever told that I was gay, and I knew that he would never tell the other guys. They may have suspected it; we did spend an awful lot of time together. But I only remember anyone asking me about it one time. Back in the early days, JY casually asked me once if I was gay. I quickly and indignantly denied it, giving my best "Duh-I-can't-believe-you're-asking-me-that" attitude. Years later, JY and I were talking about that conversation.

He said, "Why did you tell me you weren't gay when I asked you?"

I was honest. I told him that I didn't think he had the maturity to understand it at the time. Would he have been cool about it? Maybe. I don't know. But at the time it was a chance that I wasn't willing to take.

Not surprisingly, after that conversation with JY, none of the other band members brought up the issue. Maybe it never occurred to them, or maybe they just didn't care. Either way, I didn't give them much opportunity to broach the subject. Reverting back to my childhood ways, I kept quiet about my private life, stayed to myself, and contin-ued to live a safe existence under the radar.

Of course, at the time, there still wasn't much to hide. But I had begun exploring the gay community in Chicago a bit more. As I moved into my early twenties, I progressed from seeing movies in the dark to eventually going into bars where I could actually see people's faces. During the band's breaks from touring, when I was home in Chicago, I started going out a bit. I kept in touch with some of my high school buddies, who by now were more open about being gay—at least with each other. We started venturing into the city together on weekends. Going downtown was always liberating to me. It was a chance to break out of the boundaries of my old neighborhood; a chance to meet differ-ent people and have new experiences; a place where the "lights were brighter."

Even as a teenager, it was always exciting to go downtown. John and I would take the train into the city. Ironically, I remember that John and I would sometimes go to a newsstand right outside of the Randolph Street T station. It was almost a block long, with every kind of magazine imaginable. I was always attracted to the physique magazines—the ones with the muscle-bound body builders on the cover. I used to pick up a copy and flip through the pages. I enjoyed seeing the great-looking male bodies—not just in a sexual way, but also in an aesthetic way. I appreciated the male form. For some reason, this upset John.

I remember him saying, "Put that down!"

I argued back, "Why? It's a body building magazine!"

He said, "Just put it down!"

Now in my twenties, here I was not far from Randolph Station, ready to appreciate the male form in a new way.

Back in the 1970s, all the gay bars were still somewhat underground. Only a few years earlier it was not unusual for police to burst into a bar and raid it simply because a few gay men were hanging out having drinks together. They arrested patrons on "indecency" charges for kissing, holding hands, and cross-dressing. This was after the famous Stonewall riots in New York in 1969, but Chicago was still trying to figure out where it stood on the gay scene. The Midwest was extremely conservative and Chicago has one of the largest Catholic populations in the country. Both of these factors meant that Chicago was probably a bit behind other major cities in its acceptance of the gay community.

When I was twenty-two, I met a man in one of these bars and had my first gay experience. I don't know what prompted me to take that leap. I had finished college and knew that everyone else was having sex, so I guess I figured, why not? If some people remember their first experience as something wonderful, mine certainly wasn't. I suppose the first time is awkward for everyone, but as a gay man, it's even harder. There is no socialization process, no high school dating rituals to ease you into sex. There are no first kisses or fumbled attempts at getting to second base. In short, you have little idea what to do and no idea how to do it.

There was nothing magical about how I selected my first partner either. I was in a bar, and basically he picked me up. It was easy. I was drinking. He was horny. We have a match, ladies and gentlemen! The bar that we met at was far from where I lived, so I wasn't worried that anyone from my neighborhood would recognize me. An older man at the bar offered to buy me a drink. I accepted. We got to talking and he finally asked me if I wanted to go back to his place. I said, "Yes."

We left the bar and drove to the suburbs, where he lived. I don't know his story. He may even have been married. Once inside his place, I started to get a little creeped out, but it was too late to turn back. He started talking about the crewel pattern on his drapes. I remember thinking, "Go tell this to some other old geezer."

After we got together, I remember confessing to him that it was my first time.

He actually got confrontational. He said, "Yeah, right."

I was pissed, but at the same time, I thought to myself, "Hey, I must be pretty good at this."

If any good came from this experience, it was simply to give me enough confidence to say, "I deserve better than this."

Eventually, I would become much more particular about who I chose as a partner. I remember the next man I met was a ballet dancer in the Chicago ballet company. He was older too, but in a sophisticated way. He took me back to his apartment on Lake Shore Drive. I was very impressionable at the time, so this was intriguing to me. I must have asked a million questions about what he did, and where he worked, and how long he lived here. Obviously, not the kind of questioning that somebody wants in a one-night stand, but I was still new to the intricacies of gay dating rituals. I was just thrilled to get a glimpse into his world. He must have been thinking, "Who is this kid and why is he asking so many questions?"

I had a few more experiences in my early twenties, but they were few and far between. I wasn't sure that I was really ready for the more intimate aspects of gay sex, and I certainly wasn't ready for anything more than an anonymous late-night rendezvous. Each encounter was just one more chance that I might be recognized by someone I knew. So, I toned things down, and once again shifted the focus to my work.

CHAPTER SIX

ALMOST FAMOUS

Work became a constant source of distraction and enjoyment. It was also the perfect excuse to ignore my own needs and desires, and push any idea of having a personal life to the back burner. And if work wasn't enough of a distraction, I was also dealing with increasing pressure on the home front. My father's death a couple of years earlier had been very sad for my family, especially for my mother. I know my mother was extremely lonely with my father gone. My sister and brother were both married by then, so I tried to step in to fill the gap as best I could.

I ended up being my mother's primary companion and caregiver for the next twenty years of her life. Although this role was entirely self-inflicted, it didn't ease my sense of obligation. It also didn't ease the pressure. I had become the center and the focus of my mother's life, and my home life became quite oppressive in the years after my father's death. I actually welcomed the long weeks on the road with the guys where one form of privacy deprivation was swapped for another.

When I was home, however, I did my best to play the role of the good son. My mother knew almost nothing about my personal life or where I went on the weekends, and that was the way I wanted it. I believe my mother was still hoping that I was going to meet a nice girl like my brother did and get married. I saw no reason to burst her bubble.

One day when I was home on a break from the road, I got a call from a neighborhood girl named Donna. Donna was a pretty girl of Irish-Italian descent who I had initially met through my cousin. She was about five years younger than I was and I remember thinking that she was a sweet kid. Now she was graduating from high school. It seemed that she needed a date to the prom, and unbeknownst to be me, she had been harboring a secret crush on me. Needless to say, I had been oblivious to any clues that she might have sent my way. I remember my mother calling me to the phone.

"Chuck, it's that nice girl, Donna. She's on the phone for you."

As I took the call, I could see my mother hovering in the background, trying to seem like she was nonchalantly straightening up the room. I know she heard every word.

When I hung up, she looked at me. I looked back. "Well, what did she want?" I almost laughed.

"She wants me to take her to her prom."

"Oh. That's nice." I knew my mother's day was made. She loved Donna, and for the first time, she was seeing some vague hope of a future daughter-in-law. She added, "She's so mature for her age."

Donna was only eighteen-years-old at the time. Even though I was in my early twenties, I agreed to go to her prom with her with no hesitation. She really was a sweet girl, and besides, it would make my mother very happy. We ended up having a really nice time together. It was a much better experience than my own prom had been, what seemed like a lifetime ago. Donna was smart and funny, and unlike many people, she actually got my sense of humor. She was also a beautiful girl. She had dark hair and dark eyes. We actually made a very attractive couple. There was only one problem—she was straight and I was gay.

After the prom, I knew that I would see her again. I could tell that Donna really liked me, and in my own way, I liked her very much too. We started seeing each other casually. It was easy to be with her and it was even easier to be her date. Unlike seeing other men, there was no need to hide my relationship with Donna. If there was a party, I could walk in with her on my arm. And selfishly, my relationship with Donna also served as a good front. No one would suspect I was gay if I was dating a woman. I can't say that this was the reason that I started a relationship with her, but it certainly was a good fringe benefit. Besides, because I was on the road so much, things couldn't get too complicated.

Over the next year or two, Donna became part of my life. She would sometimes follow the band and came to a lot of our performances in the area. We would go to parties and out to dinner. My entire family was crazy about her. Even though John knew I was gay, he used to make jokes about what our kids would look like if Donna and I ever married, since we both had such dark Italian looks. He always teased me about having dark circles under my eyes, and he joked, "If you and Donna ever have kids, they'll be raccoons." Sometimes you just want to kill your siblings.

Of course, although I came to love Donna like a sister, or even more so, I never had the same feelings for her that I knew she had for me. Although I had never been in a real relationship with a man, I knew that there was something missing here. I knew that if and when I did have a relationship with a man, it would feel different. But at the time, I really didn't see any downside to continuing my friendship with Donna.

I thought, "It's cool. She likes being with me, I like being with her. What's wrong with that?"

But I realize now that I was being unfair to her. Donna—who did not know that I was gay—was falling in love with me.

One night, a few years into our relationship, Donna and I went out on a date. By then, I had moved out of my mother's house and had my own apartment. After dinner, Donna and I went back to my place. There was nothing all that out-of-the-ordinary about it. We sat on the couch and began kissing. We would make out like this sometimes, though I never let things progress very far. Kissing Donna was pleasant enough—not in an erotic way, but more as a means of expressing affection, and at the slight chance of feeling something sexual toward her. On this particular evening, Donna seemed like she had something on her mind.

She stopped kissing, and looked up at me. Out of the blue, she said, "Chuck, let's get married."

I was stunned and heartbroken simultaneously. I knew I was going to hurt her, but I had to be honest. I said, "Donna, I can't marry you. I'm gay."

Maybe Donna knew it all along. She stared into my eyes and said something surprising. "It doesn't matter."

"Donna, it matters to me. I can't be the husband that you need me to be," I said. Saying those words felt terrible. But I knew I would feel even worse if I continued to deceive her. Donna left my apartment in a strange mood—a little sad and a little angry. I tried calling her several times afterward, but I could not get in touch with her. About a month later, one of her relatives called and told me that Donna had gotten married to someone else.

I hoped that she hadn't rushed into something. I hoped she hadn't made a mistake. And I hoped that I wasn't the cause of it if she did. But I knew that there was nothing else that I could do, and I had to let her go. I have seen so many gay men who marry women only to cause so much anguish years later when they simply cannot continue to live a lie. After going through all the rituals of marriage, the poor woman often ends up wondering, "Did this man ever love me?" It can be devastating.

I saw one devastating example first hand. I knew a boy from the neighborhood who showed clear signs of being gay from a young age. He was kind of a soft, gentle kid. One day when we were teenagers, some friends and I went to pick him up to go out. He answered the door in his underwear. White briefs to be exact. It was provocative, but totally out of the blue and inappropriate. I said, "Uhhhh, where are your pants?" In our minds, we were all thinking, there's something different going on here.

This poor boy's father was constantly beating him up for not being the girl-chasing, football-playing son that he wanted. This kid got the shit kicked out of him his entire childhood simply for being who he was. Eventually, the boy got married very young to a beautiful young woman just to get out of his father's house. Years later, his wife discovered his secret life and tried to commit suicide. It caused so much pain for both him and the woman he married. Despite how hard it was telling Donna that I could not marry her, I was glad that I had never deceived her in this way.

Despite all the time that I spent with Donna during my twenties and the ruse that I was playing for whomever wanted to believe it, I never stopped longing for the camaraderie of other gay men. After weeks on the road focusing on work, or during weeks of spending all my free time with Donna, I was always drawn back into the bar scene. I began to discover the nuances of the different bars in the area. Some bars were casual pub-like places where you would just drink and eat. Others were poser bars, catering to good-looking young men who liked to dance and otherwise show off their wares. Others were edgier, more progressive bars, where it was not unusual to find men having sex in dark corners or in restrooms.

I'm not saying that I didn't find the latter bars intriguing, but eventually I started hanging out at a specific Old Town bar that was known as a leather-and-Levi's kind of place. You get the picture—jeans, leather vests, uniforms, and combat boots. Think the Village People without the Indian. The first time that I went there, I was scared to death. I knew I was attracted physically to the men and the way that they dressed, but I wasn't sure exactly what they were into. A huge bear of a man in leather pants and a cop hat can be a bit intimidating to a newbie. But as I worked my way into the crowd and began to hear snippets of conversations, I realized, "These guys are talking about recipes!"

Suddenly, it wasn't so scary. These were normal guys wearing costumes.

What I liked about the place was that you could actually meet someone, see his face, and have a conversation. Basically, it was a cruise bar, but if you just stood around and watched, which is what I usually did, you could observe the interaction between men. It sounds strange today, but bar settings were the only place where I could see role models of gay men relating to each other as people. Sometimes they would talk in twosomes; sometimes they would socialize in groups. Sometimes they would partner; sometimes they would walk away alone. I thought this was cool, because I finally felt that if someone approached me, I could be myself. I rarely initiated conversation, but even when I sat back and observed, I was part of something. By now, I wasn't looking for purely physical male contact, but rather to meet someone with whom I had some emotional connection. This is where I met Richard, who eventually became one of my dearest and oldest friends.

I was first attracted to Richard's looks. He was a strapping, tall, dark, and handsome type—sort of like Tom Selleck. We started out as friends, then became lovers, then went back to being pals. I wouldn't exactly call what we had a relationship. Basically, we enjoyed a hot fling, fooled around a lot, and then decided that we worked better as friends. Looking back, I know that it could have never lasted because we were both too interested in seeing what else was out there. In those days, still the pre-AIDS era, you didn't limit yourself to any one person. I was gaining some confidence in my sexuality—at least in this sheltered environment of the bars—and wanted to share my newly found fabulousness. One of the bartenders used to joke when he saw Richard and me, "Oh, here come the crowd pleasers, stand back."

This is not to say that I was becoming any less secretive about my sexual orientation in the world at large. At the time, no one knew where the gay places were in the city unless they were gay too. They were always in the dingier parts of town, hidden away from prying eyes and potential trouble. I suppose that's the way it had to be at the time, and I'm sure that's all I could have handled anyway. But the furtive nature of gay nightlife only furthered the notion that we all had something to be ashamed of.

I didn't feel that I even had the choice to come out at that time. In my mind, it would have served no purpose. I knew that being gay was a core part of my existence. I also knew that the band was a core part of me. Unfortunately, I didn't see how the two could ever meet. In my mind, if I came out and the band suffered even one less record sale, someone in the group might place the blame on me. I didn't want to be in that position. I wasn't only jeopardizing my own career; I was responsible for the livelihood of four other guys. So, as the band become more successful, the pressure to stay undercover only got worse.

In the bars, I would never mention that I was a musician or even in a band. Of course, even if I had, few people would have heard of Styx in the mid-1970s. As we became more well-known, however, it became more difficult to hide. All my good friends were very protective of me because of my career, and never let on that I was any different from anyone else. One time a bartender who I had gotten to know pretty well called me out.

He said, "Hey, Chuck, I saw you on TV the other day." He smiled slyly waiting to see my response.

I wasn't going to deny it. I stayed cool. "Oh yeah, what did you think?"

"You were all covered up. Sunglasses and shit. You looked like Super Fly. Were you trying to hide up there?"

I said, "Hide? No, why would I? The hat and sunglasses are just my idea of fashion." I believed it at the time.

All these years later, I realize he may have been on to something.

CHAPTER SEVEN

HEY NOW,
YOU'RE A ROCK STAR

Good things began to happen in 1975. Eventually. After "Lady" rose up the charts, we enjoyed a brief taste of success. Soon enough, though, we were back to playing the same gigs in the same places that we had played before our top-ten hit. We thought, "Wait a minute. We have a gold record and six months later, it's over. There's something wrong here."

It didn't take long to realize that the problem was our record label. While we had originally liked the idea of signing with a hometown label, it was evident that a Chicago-based label was not going to cut it if we ever wanted to make it as a major player. The pulses of the recording industry were on the East and West Coasts and that's where we needed to be.

After the success of "Lady," we were approached by several major record labels. We took the opportunity to go label shopping. After hearing all of their proposals, we decided to sign with A&M Records out in Los Angeles. A&M's Herb Alpert and Jerry Moss had a reputation for being two of the classiest guys in the business. After getting to know them, I agreed. As musicians themselves, the music really did come first at their record company. They had a true commitment to their artists.

The 1970s was A&M's Golden Age. The label was buzzing with talent and great producers. Some of the artists with A&M around that time included Joe Cocker, Peter Frampton, Supertramp, Carole King, Cat Stevens, The Tubes, Quincy Jones, and the Carpenters. Visiting their offices in the old Charlie Chaplin Studios near Sunset Boulevard and La Brea Avenue in Hollywood, we were struck by the professionalism of everyone we met. A&M didn't necessarily offer us the best deal in terms of royalties, but we felt it was the best place for our long-term growth.

We signed with A&M in 1975 and got our first good manager. While Vince had tried his best, our new manager, Derrick, opened us up to a whole new world. He had worked with a lot of other international rock bands before and didn't quite know what to make of Styx when he first met us. I remember the first time he went to John's house, he said, "I never met a rock star with a clean apartment." He was shocked that we all lived relatively normal lives. While others may have had their problems with Derrick through the years, I say any manager who could bring a rock band from the South Side of Chicago to the top of the industry in a few short years had to know what he was doing.

As soon as we joined the new label we went to work on our first album, *Equinox*. One of the cuts from the albums, the up-tempo rock song "Lorelei," shot up the charts, reaching #27 on the pop charts. We were on our way again. The cover art for *Equinox* showed a big cube of ice on fire. To me, that illustration symbolized Wooden Nickel melting away and a new phase of our career beginning.

In the fall, we went on tour to promote the new album. We were all pretty excited to be out touring, promoting our first album with A&M. We had two hits now in our repertoire, "Lady" and "Lorelei," and we would get tremendous fan reaction when we played them. It was a high. But soon into the tour it became increasingly apparent that John Curulewski was having a difficult time. He was becoming more and more depressed and none of us really knew why. We knew that he was having problems with some of the creative decisions that others in the band were making. JC really was an artist and had a lot of strong ideas. I don't think any of us really knew how unhappy he was. By November, he decided that he had had enough. JC announced that he was leaving the band to spend more time with his family. It's unfortunate that after sticking with the band through the difficult years, JC left us just as we were on the brink of hitting it big. At the time, though, none of us knew what the next few years were going to bring. We didn't begrudge JC. He needed to do what was right for him. But with the band in the middle of our first tour with our new record label, that left us in a bit of a lurch. We needed a new guitarist—fast.

Our tour manager had a suggestion. He had seen a band called MS Funk playing in the Chicago area and was very impressed with their lead singer/guitarist. He suggested that we call him in for an audition. Somehow they tracked him down and he agreed to come and play for us. So, we all got together at Dennis's house and in walks Tommy Shaw. He had long blonde hair, bangs, a southern accent and he looked very young. We didn't quite know what to make of him. But as soon as he started jamming and singing with us, we kind of knew right away that he was the one. When he nailed the high note in the chorus of Lady, which JC had always sung, the deal was sealed. We welcomed Tommy to the band, and Styx was born in the incarnation that I believe most people remember as the classic line up: Dennis DeYoung, James Young, Chuck and John Panozzo, and Tommy.

Tommy was young—twenty-two years old to be exact—with the boyish good looks that were so popular in the mid-1970s. He was the total marketing package—talent and looks. There was never any doubt that he would attract a new demographic to the band—mainly in the form of young women. Soon we started appearing on the cover of magazines like *Tiger Beat* and *16 Magazine*. We would give Tommy a hard time about his cheesecake image, of course, but that kind of exposure was definitely good for the band. We also respected him as a musician. It was unfortunate that JC left the band, but when someone leaves, all you can do is try to replace him with someone just as good or better. We got that in Tommy.

Tommy is also a great songwriter, and our first album after he joined the band was actually titled after one of his songs, *Crystal Ball*. Some of our best work came out of that period. It's hard to believe that the band actually produced such great, cohesive albums considering how different all our styles were. Dennis was all about theatrical ballads. JY was heavy metal. And now Tommy brought a Rockabilly background to the group. But when we would all get in a room with our instruments, somehow it would come together. A song would be presented, and we would all start getting used to it and putting our own arrangements into it. We instinctively knew when everything started clicking.

It was a challenge for John and me to adjust our styles to match the songwriter since all three were so different. We really had to make sure that a song ended up the way that the songwriter wanted it to sound. Each person had a different style of writing. Sometimes, one of them would bring a song to the group virtually complete. In those cases, you could get it right away and just focus on adding the nuances. Other times, someone would show up with an idea that was very loose. Sometimes I would look at John and think, "Where's the song in this song?" But we tried really hard to get it right and for the most part, we succeeded. If we didn't respect each other's style and collaborate in this way, I don't think the songs would have been hits.

Soon after Tommy joined the band, things really began to pick up momentum. Under A&M's direction, we were advised that if we wanted to build our following by playing for really large audiences, we were going to have to start playing the opening act for some of the popular bands of the day. Although it was humbling to be the act that no one in the stadium paid money to see, we recognized that it was a smart move. The opportunity for exposure is huge, and if there is a good fit between the openers and the main act, there is a lot of potential to attract new fans.

With the power of A&M behind us, Styx went on to become the opening act for some of the hottest rock bands around at the time. Over the years, we played with KISS, ZZ Top, David Bowie, Frank

Zappa, Three Dog Night, Blue Oyster Cult, The Doobie Brothers, Bad Company, and Aerosmith. While we always had aspirations of becoming the main event, this experience gave us the poise to eventually command the attention of an arena of 30,000 people.

I think one of Styx's strong suits was that we were a great live band. All the practice touring and playing over the years had really paid off. We started opening for bigger and bigger acts, and playing bigger and bigger venues. A&M also introduced us to the Canadian market, which became one of our strongest fan bases. We knew we were on our way when we went to Canada to play the opening act for Bad Company. The fan reaction to our music was incredible. In fact, we ended up getting a bigger response from the crowd than they did. This scenario repeated itself again and again with many of the acts that we fronted.

In short, we started to become a nightmare of an opening act for the featured artists because we often got a more enthusiastic reception than they did. It got to the point where no one wanted us to open for them anymore. This ended up being a good thing. That's when we stopped being the opening act and became "the act."

By the time we started headlining our own concerts, we had performed in front of so many people that we were totally at ease on stage. It was exciting rather than nerve-racking. By now we also had a few hit songs, so we would look out and see the audience singing along to the lyrics. It's an amazing feeling to think that people actually took time out of their lives to learn the words to our music. The adulation and sound of the crowd can be overwhelming, but the idea is to perform like you're performing for one person. Whether you're performing for 3 people or 30,000, you have to be 100 percent there.

By the end of 1976, we started to take some time off from our touring schedule to record our third album for A&M. We released *The Grand Illusion* on July 7th, 1977—7-7-77. Although clearly a marketing ploy by the record company, the date certainly turned out to be lucky for us. It raced up the charts. The singles "Come Sail Away,"

"Fooling Yourself," and "Miss America" all made the charts. *The Grand Illusion* was our first album to go platinum. It represented a turning point in our careers and in our lives.

In many ways, *The Grand Illusion* was our best album—or at least it was the album that represented Styx working at its best artistically. Of all our albums, I would say that this one was truly our most collaborative effort. JY, Dennis, and Tommy all contributed to the songwriting. John was at his best as a musician, not yet plagued by the addictive demons that he would eventually have to battle. And I was able to blend my music and my love of art by working on the album's cover art.

A graphic designer helped me adapt a beautiful print from the surrealist painter René Magritte. I wanted the artwork to capture the mystical, spiritual quality of the album, and I was very proud of the end product. I remember bringing a mock-up of the album cover to the other guys and asking, "What do you think?"

Never short on opinions, they started to make all kinds of suggestions and critiques. I listened politely and said, "Thanks for your input. I'll take that into consideration. But this is the album cover." That wasn't my style, but I felt that strongly about it. And I think it was the right choice. I think anyone who has ever owned the album can still picture the cover. It was a wonderful piece of art and an illusion in itself.

The Grand Illusion started the ball rolling. It was the first of four consecutive triple-platinum albums. With each album after its release, we just kept getting stronger and stronger. In 1978, we released *Pieces of Eight* with "Renegade" and "Blue Collar Man," followed by *Cornerstone* in 1979 with the single "Babe," which hit #1 and became our highest-reaching single of all time. And finally in 1981, we released *Paradise Theatre* and became the first rock band in history to achieve four triple-platinum albums. Today, many albums go triple platinum, but at the time it was quite an accomplishment. We produced so many hits during that relatively brief period—"Come Sail Away," "Fooling Yourself," "Babe," "Renegade," "Best of Times," and "Too Much Time on My Hands." There are about twenty songs from that era that hit the charts.

Life during this period was something of a blur that can only be fully appreciated in retrospect. By age thirty, I was living a life that most people only dream of living. But it's a strange phenomenon. When you're caught in the whirlwind, it begins to feel commonplace. Suddenly, you begin to forget all the years of walking through the kitchen to play the wedding. You forget the people throwing quarters at you on some makeshift stage. It all becomes a distant memory. You feel elevated. People treat you differently. Now that you can afford things, you seem to get a lot of things for free. The guitar strings that I used to buy—free. The guitar itself—free. Clothes, sneakers, tennis rackets—you name it, we were being offered it. Now that we had a best-selling album and were a household name, everyone wanted us to use their brand of whatever. It was crazy.

The money wasn't bad either after all those years of eating every other day and sleeping four to a room. I remember when we got our first big royalty check. The business manager that we had used for years called John and I and said, "Come see me, I have a check for you both."

When John and I went to see him, he handed us both an envelope. I opened mine first and looked inside. When I saw the amount, I said, "Oh, this can't be for us."

I asked, John, "How much is yours?"

He said, "Two hundred and fifty thousand dollars. How much is yours?"

I said, "Two hundred and fifty thousand."

All we could do was laugh. This was crazy money to us. When we started out I remember thinking, if I could make $50,000 at this I'll be happy. Now, it looked like we were going to make a little bit more.

I didn't spend elaborately when we started making money. But I did have my little splurges. For instance, I bought a Jaguar. I remember the Jaguar salesman warning me, "Now are you sure you want to buy this car? I don't want you spending all your money."

Eventually, I also bought a condo in downtown Chicago, but when I first got the car, I still lived at home. So here was this brand-new Jaguar parked in the driveway of my mother's little tract house in South Holland, Illinois (by this time she had moved from Roseland). The car was worth more than everything in the house combined—maybe even the house itself.

Life on the road changed quite a bit too since the days of sitting backward in the rented station wagon. When we first started to become successful, the rented vehicles were replaced with buses. Our equipment went on trucks. And this time around, we had a road crew to set up and take down the instruments. The Holiday Inn was replaced by places like the Beverly Wilshire and the Ritz-Carlton. With time, the buses were replaced with commercial jets and eventually our own plane with "Styx" painted on the side.

Looking back on our roots in the South Side of Chicago, it was particularly astounding to my brother and me that we had become so successful. Most of the men from our neighborhood grew up to be factory workers, and here we were performing to stadium crowds. I was living a life that I could hardly comprehend. When I went off to work, I would take the elevator down from my luxury high-rise, get into a limousine, and be driven up to the tarmac of our private plane. Then, I'd get out of the car, and step onto the red carpet and climb on board.

Inside we had our own pilot and co-pilot—nice guys whom we liked a lot. We also had our own stewardess, whom we harassed unmercifully. For one thing, we wouldn't listen to a thing that she told us to do. We'd immediately start quizzing her on what kind of food they had for us that night, and asking for wine or beer or soda. When things were good with the band, there was usually a fair amount of joking and talking on board until everyone went their separate ways and fell asleep or read.

When we touched down, there was usually a group of young people waiting for the plane. They would find out the tour schedule and come to wait for us to arrive. Of course, many of the fans who came to wait for us were women. You could count on that. There were certain women who would follow the group from city to city. Others would be local girls who liked Styx, or who liked the rock scene in general. In the beginning, the number of women (or girls, it was sometimes hard to tell their age) who turned out for our performances surprised me. In time, though, you just expected it. The faces began to blur together from city to city, and for all I knew, it could have been the same group of fifty or so scantily clad women who were transported and plopped down in front of the stage door in each different city.

Most of them never made it beyond the back door. The lucky ones found a way to get backstage passes. But even the ones allowed backstage rarely got attention from any of the guys in the band. After a certain point, it just gets a little monotonous—even if you're straight and single. If you're married, or worse yet, gay, it gets old very quickly. This meant that our road crew got very lucky, very often. If the girls couldn't get to anyone in the band, the roadies were the next best thing. And the roadies were never too busy or too tired to take one for the team. In exchange, the girls got access to hang out backstage while Styx performed. Everyone seemed happy enough with the system.

While reading some old articles to jog my memory for this book, I came across an article in the *Chicago Sun-Times* by Rick Kogan, a reporter who traveled with Styx for a few concert dates in 1979. I remember him. When we played the Long Beach Civic Center's 12,000-seat sports arena in California, he rode in the car with JY and me as we approached the stadium. His recounting of the scene made me smile. It's also a great snapshot of what life was like for us back in the day. The article from 1980 was called, "The Band That Styx It To 'Em." Here's what he wrote:

"At once, a sleek, gray Cadillac limousine glides toward the back stage area. Small groups of girls rush from under trees and other hiding places like a pack of lions attacking an antelope.

They bang on the windows, try to halt the driver's progress by standing in front of the car. They are a desperate bunch. Rain soaks their makeup and ruins their clothes. Some are crying.

"Tommy, Tommmmmmmmmy! I love you!" one girl yells as she bangs against the limousine's window.

Inside the gray limousine, James Young, the tall, blond guitarist for Styx who likes to be called J.Y. looks out the window.

"It sure is raining," he says. Next to him, bass player Chuck Panozzo, finishing the last part of a cover story on Styx in a recent issue of Record World magazine, nods his head in agreement. Then he chuckles, and says, "They think you're Tommy."

"I'm not Tommy Shaw," J.Y. screams. "I'm Rod Stewart."

"Tommy, Tommmmmmmmmy! I love you! I love you!" the girl persists, now trying desperately to jump on the hood of the slippery auto.

"Oh brother," sighs J.Y. And the limousine rolls through the now fully raised backstage door and he hurries to get out and head for the dressing room.

This scene is repeated twice, as two more limousines make their way into the stadium, five and ten minutes later.

The second car carries young guitarist Tommy Shaw, drummer John Panozzo and his wife Debbie. The groupies muster their greatest energy for this car. As the youngest member of Styx and because of his good looks and flowing blond hair, Tommy Shaw is extremely popular with young girls. Some of his fans are now demonstrating their affection by covering his car with their bodies.

John and Debbie Panozzo pay no attention to the frenzy. Tommy Shaw merely smiles, and shortly all of them are inside the sports arena dressing room. By the time the last and final car appears, spectacularly black in the California rain, the groupies' enthusiasm has waned. Most of them have started tiptoeing through the puddles back to their hiding places to regroup for the band's departure in a couple of hours."

Tommy usually got the lion's share of attention from our female fans. He had the non-threatening looks that young girls love. At the time, a lot of the popular music idols looked like Ken dolls. Remember, this was the decade of Leif Garrett and David Cassidy. Girls went for the flowing blond hair, slim physiques, and pretty-boy looks. Tommy fit that mold perfectly. But none of us in the band was spared the female attention. Any of us could have had female companionship any night of the week on the road. Of course, I always tried to stay aloof to the whole thing, acting above it all.

I was always polite to the groupies. At the time, I would auto-graph whatever they wanted me to sign—bras, underwear, body parts. But as the girls in the audience were exposing their breasts and throwing their underwear on stage, I was more interested in their tight-jeaned boyfriends standing next to them with the skinny hips and no shirts. Sometimes I would even get a little annoyed. One time a woman was trying desperately to get my attention at the end of a show. She was yelling, "Chuck, Chuck. Give me back my under-wear." I saw what she was talking about . . . there were a pair of panties lying on the stage. I went over, picked up the garment and held it between my fingers.

I said, "This is what you want?"

She said, "Yes, I threw them. Throw them back."

I said, "No. You throw your underwear on stage, they belong to the crew."

I don't know why I singled out this woman. The whole thing just got too silly for me. So while the rest of the guys were hanging bras off their instruments, I was doing my best above-it-all act, thinking, "I'm not into that nonsense. I'm a musician."

Because of this, my persona on stage was much darker than the other guys. I always had a dark, brooding look. Thanks to my Italian heritage, I was the kid who could grow a mustache at age fourteen, and I wore a beard in Styx's early days. In some ways, I used my physi-cal appearance like a deflector. I played it. Ironically, this aloof aura only served to make me more mysterious to some of our female fans. Although I was the least threatening person on stage, I looked like the tough guy. It made me laugh; if only they knew the whole story. So it became an act for me, and I hid behind this image of strength.

Despite our rising fame, some things about life on the road hadn't changed all that dramatically from the early days. We traveled better and stayed in nicer hotels—the days of sharing rooms and living on pizzas were over—but I still felt the same sense of isolation from the other guys. In actuality, it was probably worse. The more successful we became, the less time we seemed to spend together on any kind of interpersonal level. Three of the guys were married and Dennis had a child, so we didn't do much socializing on the road.

Not that it was *all* serious business though. With John around, that would have been almost impossible. He had the ability to break the tension in even the most stressful situations. And he was always playing pranks. John was a great physical comedian in the tradition of Jackie Gleason or John Belushi. I used to tell him, forget about the drums, you should do standup. Of course, he could never really have been a comedian because he would only show his humor to those he felt comfortable around. In the early days, this meant that I was the brunt of most of his practical jokes. I remember one time as kids we were all out back roasting marshmallows. I said, "John, give me a marshmallow."

Before I knew what was happening, he placed a flaming marshmallow in the palm of my hand. I started screaming.

"Daaaaad! Daaaad! John put a flaming marshmallow in my hand!"

I suppose my parents were used to the drill by now. "Well, why the hell did you take it?" was my father's only reply.

I glared at my brother. John, ever the innocent, shrugged, "You said you wanted a marshmallow."

At least on the road, I got to share his abuse with the other guys. If you kept your mouth open too long, John would drop his smoked cigarette in it. If you fell asleep in your seat at the airport, he'd tape you to your chair with rock 'n' roll tape. Rock 'n' roll tape—which is like duct tape that the crew uses to hold wires down—was always dangerous in John's hands. One time he got the whole band to help grab our tour manager—who was a huge hulk of a guy—and duct tape him to a table.

But despite the breaks of levity and the superstar treatment, life on the road is hard. Days of little sleep, bad eating habits, too much partying, and odd hours wear you down. Quite honestly, it can all become a bit of a grind. So, when we didn't have to be together, we weren't. During the day, if we arrived in a city early, John and I might go out to lunch and visit some local attractions or check out the record shops. Since we usually were up until two or three in the morning after a show, sometimes I would just nap. Tommy liked to work out. Dennis hung out with his family. We would all go off to do our own thing and would meet up again around four or five o'clock when it was time to leave for the show.

On free nights, the other guys would often go out to dinner with their wives and girlfriends, either as a group or in couples. Sometimes I would go, but often I would be the third wheel and either wouldn't be included in the plans, or would be so obviously out of place that I would turn them down.

I wasn't longing for more nights out together. What I was missing was a sense of camaraderie on the road. There's a certain amount of male bonding that happens between straight men during what I call "locker room talk," and I wasn't part of that. When the band members and the stagehands would hang out together, the conversations often flowed to sex and getting laid—especially as our legion of female fans began to grow. But the things that would make the other guys laugh—a female fan lifting up her shirt, a pair of panties thrown on stage—just didn't do it for me. I couldn't really participate in that kind of banter. So when we were together on the road, I would let the other guys dominate the conversations. I wasn't a chick guy. I wasn't a sports guy. I had nothing to add, so I just sat back and listened. I'm sure the other guys noticed that I acted different than they did, but I think it was dismissed as, "Oh, that's just Chuck being Chuck."

To find any sort of male connection on the road, I would have to hit the gay bars. This was risky business in a strange city, so it took me a while to get up the confidence to start going out. It also took a lot of energy. First, I had to find the bars. Not an easy task if you couldn't risk asking anyone where they were located. So I had to be creative. Sometimes I would pick up a local gay newspaper and look for advertisements. One time I spotted two men together who looked gay, and simply followed them. I thought, "They'll lead you where you want to go." Sure enough, they did.

Then I'd have to figure out how I would get there and get back without being seen. Not that anyone really cared what the others were up to. The other guys never noticed where I went anyway. But I still treated every excursion like a CIA mission.

Usually, once I got to the bar, I just enjoyed talking to other gay men and being able to act and speak freely. But occasionally, I would hook up with somebody and bring them back to my hotel. Back in the late 1970s and early 1980s, before we even knew about the threat of AIDS, one-night stands were not a big deal. The only fear was of getting caught. After these furtive outings, I would make sure that I snuck back to the hotel before anybody might start looking for me.

My personal life on the road consisted of a series of one-night stands with guys who I didn't even tell my true identity. I rarely told them my full name or that I was in town with Styx. Of course, even if I had, most gay men probably would have had no idea what I did for a living. It was my perception that not one gay man I knew cared much about rock 'n' roll. While I spent my life entrenched in the rock arena, an entirely different musical genre—disco—was taking the club scene and the gay community by storm. For my part, I didn't care much about disco divas like Donna Summer or Gloria Gaynor, or even the gay disco artists like Sylvester or Boys Town Gang. I was completely out of the pop music culture scene that was playing out at gay nightclubs across the country. Instead of dancing in clubs, I was working throughout most of the 1970s, rendering the gap between the gay community and me even larger.

My professional life was clearly on the rise, but personally, I was growing further out of touch with my true self. Yet, I wasn't ready to do anything to close that rift. In fact, after Styx became more popular, I was plagued with the fear of being outed. I asked myself, "Do you want to be out and give up your career, or do you want to keep playing with the band?" As I saw it then, those were my choices. Obviously, my decision was to keep the status quo.

To ease my own conscience, I made a few halfhearted attempts to support the gay community. For instance, when AIDS first became a health crisis in the early 1980s, I marched over to the Howard Brown Clinic in Chicago and gave $5,000 for AIDS research. I didn't even really know what AIDS was at the time, but I told the receptionist, "I want to donate this money because I know there is an STD out there that is killing our community." She asked if I would like to list my name as a donor in their development brochure. I told her that it was not necessary.

Now, I look back and think what a coward I was. I tried to pretend that I was simply being selfless by giving an anonymous donation. In actuality, I was afraid that someone would see my name and put the pieces together.

Instances like this still shame me. I know now that I should have been in solidarity with the gay community. But back then, being in the public eye, I couldn't take that step. Many of my buddies who I grew up with felt the same way, and they weren't even rock stars. Men of my generation knew that being gay could be a death sentence. You could lose your job. You could lose your reputation. You could lose everything.

So, during this period, I made my life all about Styx. My personal life consisted of encounters in the dark in random cities, and on weekends at home, going out to bars with my buddies. That was it. But you can't hide behind your work forever, or as they say, all good things must come to an end. What I didn't know at the time was that this was going to happen sooner than I had planned.

III
FREE-FALLING

CHAPTER EIGHT

BREAKING UP
IS HARD TO DO

In 1980, Styx hit a milestone. We had our first #1 single. Ironically, this momentous event began to loosen the thread that eventually led to the complete unraveling of the band. Here's how it happened.

After releasing the album *Pieces of Eight* in 1978, which produced the hits "Renegade" and "Blue Collar Man," we began work on our next album for A&M called *Cornerstone*. When the album was almost completed, Dennis slipped in a last-minute addition—a love song to his wife Suzanne titled "Babe." I remember the first time Dennis brought the song to the group. You could see the look of horror as JY and Tommy began playing this straight-up love ballad. It clearly didn't fit with their rocker sensibilities, and quite honestly, it was a departure from anything that Styx had ever done in the past. We may have tested the pop-ballad waters a bit with songs like "Lady," but nothing this extreme.

But Dennis had written the song, and sang the song, and he was adamant about putting it on the album. He truly believed that this was going to be our biggest hit yet. I think the rest of us were thinking, "OK, so it might be a hit, but at what price to our reputation? Do we really want to tread into easy-listening territory?"

Eventually, Dennis got his way; it wasn't worth the energy needed to fight him. We ended up adding a bridge to the song to infuse a little bit more of the Styx harmonies into it, and put it on the *Cornerstone* album.

As it turns out, Dennis was right. In the winter of 1980, "Babe" hit #1 on the charts. Despite its success, all of us, with the exception of Dennis, saw the song as a double-edged sword. It introduced us to a new, broader audience, but it also changed the way that some of our core fans viewed the band. Rock guys like Tommy and JY had trouble with this. They struggled between appreciating the success and the money that a song like "Babe" brought us, and what they saw as compromising their artistic integrity. At one point, tensions within the group escalated so high that we actually asked Dennis to leave the band.

The split, however, was short-lived and hushed over in the press. Considering the success that we were having, it was hard to take too lofty an artistic stance. The public were digging us. We won a People's Choice award in 1981 and a Gallup poll showed that we were the most popular band in the country. After a brief cooling-off period, we asked Dennis to come back. He did—albeit with a bit more of an edge.

At this point, despite the success that Styx was experiencing, I think we all knew that it was only a matter of time until the next implosion. Tensions were just too high. When one's ego begins to eclipse one's talent, it's a problem. It is difficult to single out any one person to place all the blame on. It takes two (or more) to have an argument. However, most of the conflicts involved a common figure. Fueled by the huge commercial success of "Babe," there was a shift that occurred in the band. There was a pretense of democracy, but there was clearly a pecking order, with Dennis perched on the top branch. The only exception came when it was time to pay the bills— then we were all equal.

Despite the tension, we all began work on another album, *Paradise Theater*, in 1981. This was Dennis's brainchild. I believe the group allowed Dennis to take charge once again for several reasons: It was an attempt at reconciliation after asking him to leave. Despite the artistic differences in the group, Dennis did have a knack at producing hits; and, honestly, we thought the idea was kind of cool.

Paradise Theater was a "concept album," loosely based on an old movie theatre in Chicago. Dennis equated the theatre with America. He suggested that just like the theatre, America may have lost its luster, but was still a great country. The nation had just been through some difficult times in the early 1980s. Reagan had just won the election, the Iranian hostage crisis ended twenty minutes after his inauguration, and Americans were primed for a new wave of patriotism. The album seemed to resonate with the mood of the country, and again, we had a triple-platinum album on our hands.

We were all happy that the album was a success. But once again, Dennis had led the group further away from our rock roots. Tommy put a track on the album at the last minute, the classic "Too Much Time On My Hands," and JY wrote the song "Snowblind," but all in all, *Paradise Theater* was mostly Dennis's creation—a big, bombastic, theatrical album. The stress within the band was percolating, just looking for a reason to boil over.

Our next album, the rock opera *Kilroy Was Here*, gave us that reason. While *Paradise Theater* was an album held together around a loose conceptual theme, there was still room for individual expression, and each member of the band still had the opportunity to contribute. *Kilroy*, however, was more like a theatrical play—and every song on the album had to follow the "plot line." This perfectly suited Dennis's dream of performing in the theatre, but it did not sit well with the rest of us. In my opinion, we were rock musicians, not Broadway performers. As Tommy put it, "I just couldn't sit down and write songs about robots."

In essence, *Kilroy Was Here* was a statement on censorship and the evils of a technology-driven society. Dr. Kilroy (Dennis) is framed for murder by Dr. Righteous (JY) and his censorship-loving gang—me and John. Ultimately, Tommy, playing Jonathan Chance, proves Dr. Kilroy's innocence and sets him free. It was crazy stuff. The concert opened with a movie clip setting up the Kilroy story. We all wore futuristic-looking costumes. It was very difficult—and demeaning—to be turned from musicians into character actors. Of course, when I expressed my concerns to Dennis, he answered with the classic line, "There are no small parts, only small actors."

I thought to myself the equally classic line, "Go to hell."

There was a lot of passive-aggressive behavior going on at that point. We were all guilty. We were all acting out. I named my character in the *Kilroy* production, Lt. Vanish, because I felt I was slowly vanishing from the group. My brother and I were becoming pawns in the ongoing artistic feud between Dennis, Tommy, and to a lesser degree, JY. We were turning into day players, and I felt our value as musicians was being diminished.

I know my brother felt that way too. In classic John style, he showed it in his own unique way. During the *Kilroy* tour, we were scheduled to perform at Texas Jam in Dallas. Texas Jam was a typical hard rock festival. The fans wanted to drink beer, smoke some weed, take their clothes off—it was all about freedom and rebellion. It was also hot as hell that day.

So there we are with the other bands, Ted Nugent, and the others, getting ready to perform. We had all decided that this was not the venue to perform *Kilroy* for a variety of self-explanatory reasons. We were going to stick to our rock roots for this one. But, when we looked up at the board, we saw that there had been a last-minute change. We were scheduled to perform the Mr. Roboto shtick in broad daylight, in 90-degree heat, in front of several thousand drunken head bangers being hosed off by the security guys. Oh-kay.

Just as we take the stage, I look back at John, who I see nonchalantly slip a brown paper bag over his head with two eyeholes cut out, and proceeds to play the entire set wearing the bag. It was one of the funniest things I'd ever seen my brother do, and it perfectly typifies the frustration that was going on within the band at that time.

To Dennis's credit, I must admit that *Kilroy* was original, and as artists you do need to take risks. And, commercially, the album was fairly successful. The *Kilroy Was Here* album sold two million copies and the song "Mr. Roboto" rose to #3 on the charts. However, such an extreme departure from our roots ended up alienating many of our fans—and not inconsequentially, many of the band members.

On top of the hostility it was creating within the group, the *Kilroy* tour was plagued with difficulties of both the financial and technical variety. We were losing money by foregoing stadium dates in favor of playing smaller venues, which were better suited to the theatrical nature of the show. And technical production problems frequently forced us to cancel our appearances all together. We had never done that in twenty years of performing. It disturbed me that we had to disappoint our fans—who had spent their money to see us—simply because our stage props weren't working right.

I began to ask, "When did our act become about the props rather than the music?" After all these years, there was the clear sense that Styx was falling apart.

We all had our own way of coping. Tommy—at his own admission—helped deal with his problems by self-medicating. He got wrapped up with drugs, alcohol, and partying. John, too, was no stranger to the bottle at this point. I coped by disengaging. At times, I wouldn't even come on stage until it was my turn to play. When Dennis would go off on one of his fifteen-minute soliloquies, I would literally set down my bass on the stage and go sit in the wings. And JY, always the mediator, tried to act as the buffer between this clearly dysfunctional group. In time, he got beat up with the rest of us.

The fun ended when Tommy got his own record deal and left the band. Dennis didn't want to replace him, saying that he was worried about protecting the integrity of the band. He worried about our integrity until he too received his own solo record deal, and then said sayonara. The bitter end came on a snowy night, flying back to Chicago on our private plane. As we walked off the tarmac, we all said goodbye with one finger pointed up to the stormy sky.

It was 1984. Tommy had a record deal. Dennis had a record deal. John, JY, and I were in our mid-thirties and out of a job. We had just finished the *Kilroy* tour—which lost a lot of money—and basically we were left high and dry. When you're thirty-six and no longer part of one of the most successful rock bands in history, what do you do? What, that is, besides go into a depression that lasted about seven years.

At the time, I thought my life was over, as I simply couldn't see many options. I couldn't go back to teaching. I didn't want to join another band. After founding Styx, my ego wouldn't allow it. But looking ahead, I estimated that I had about forty more years ahead of me—that was a lot of space to fill up.

I think a lot of people fantasize about this kind of opportunity. For instance, what would happen if they won the lottery and didn't have to work any more? In a sense, I was living that kind of scenario. We had made a lot of money at a young age, and if I invested wisely, I could have lived out a fairly comfortable life without ever working another day. But like the old saying, "Careful what you wish for because it might come true," this life of leisure is not the wonderful ride that most people expect it to be. For one thing, having endless time on your hands tends to bring out the demons in people. The pitfalls are different for everyone. For John, it was drinking. For me, it was anxiety, depression, and loneliness.

The rest of the population—at least the under-seventy crowd—usually has day jobs. So there aren't many people around to play with from nine to five. The daytime has a rhythm all its own. You have a sense that there is a lot of activity going on around you—but you're not a part of it. You see store clerks and restaurant workers doing their jobs. You see people in suits and briefcases rushing off to God knows where. You see service people and cops and meter readers busy doing their thing. But you reside among the day people. The day people are that strange band of folk who include the elderly, moms with young children, the disenfranchised free spirits who think working a day job is somehow beneath them—and, of course, unemployed rock stars. It gets old fast.

So, I tried to fill my life with distraction. Whatever interested me, I would do. I became the king of adult education. I started self-study groups. I learned jazz bass. I am even a proud graduate of the American Flower Academy. In fact, I was so good at flower arranging, the females in the class hated me. I told them, "I'm an art teacher. Learn the color wheel and your arrangements might look this good too."

In addition to my assorted hobbies, I also focused a lot of attention on my family. I had been on the road for so long that, at age thirty-six, I had never taken enough time to develop meaningful relationships outside of my immediate family. My mother, brother, and sister were still the most intense relationships in my life. Now, with plenty of time on my hands, my family's dysfunction became another of my pastimes. My mother, who was getting older, enjoyed having her doting son back in Chicago on a full-time basis. I obliged her whims, taking her shopping and visiting regularly.

My brother also took up a lot of my time. Soon after the band broke up, I began to realize that his depression was even worse than mine. While I missed the band, I could have lived off of my royalties and my business investments until I eventually found another source of fulfillment. But my brother was a musician above all else. Music was a part of his being, and he had no reason to play anymore. He was lost. Even though he had a wife and child, John was having difficulty finding a reason to get up in the morning. It's a terrible thing to incur in one's life.

The band and the touring schedule had also provided the structure that someone with John's temperament needed desperately. I think that's true for many artists. Left to his own devices, John would inevitably find ways to get himself into trouble. This is when John's downward cycle of alcohol abuse and addiction first began. As a result, his marriage began to suffer. I started to spend as much time as I could with John, hoping that somehow I could help him through some of his pain.

Of course, once again, I had found the perfect setup to hide from my own pain. I was clearly repeating behavior from my past, trying to redeem myself by being the best boy in the world. But I wasn't a boy; I was a man. The codependency that I had with my mother and brother was destructive for all of us. By focusing all my time on others, I didn't have to think as much about my own issues.

But in the end, these distractions were not strong enough or fulfilling enough to fill the emptiness that I felt inside. The present sucked. And at that time, I wasn't ready to think about the future yet. So, I began obsessing about the past. I kept repeating the events of the band's breakup over and over in my head. I would replay conversations in my head and wish that I had said this or that. I would get angry with the other band members for not fighting harder to keep things together. I would get angry with myself for not having the solution that could have kept things together for everyone. But mostly I was just angry at life. I was constantly fighting against the memories, until finally I realized, "You don't have to live this way."

It was hard to flounder for such a long time, but eventually I realized that despite my best efforts to prove otherwise, I was surviving. I wasn't going to wither away and die. I wasn't going to go insane. There wasn't going to be any dramatic episode that would magically transform my existence for better or worse. In all likelihood, I would keep on living this same, miserable existence for the foreseeable future. When I finally recognized this, I thought, "OK, if you're going to keep on living, you might as well figure out the next step in your life. Styx is over. What now?"

Without Styx to hide behind, I had lost a refuge of sorts, but I also gained something else—freedom. For years, I had convinced myself that one of the reasons I was so closeted was that I could hurt my career: lose fans, lose money, lose everything. But now I had to face the reality. "Who cares if someone finds out that you're gay and in Styx—there is no more Styx."

Of course, I did not have total freedom because of the self-imposed pressures of my family and the pressures of society at large. I still wasn't ready to come out and make my voice known, but at least I felt that I didn't have as much to lose. In fact, I had everything to gain. The collapse of Styx forced me to realize the sacrifices that I had made and just how little I had to show for it in terms of what really mattered in life.

There was no question that I had a lot of toys. Since the age of thirty, I had been driving around in a 450SL Mercedes convertible and living in a luxury high-rise with views of Lake Michigan. At the time, it seemed normal, like everyone lived that way. My life had been fast-forwarded at such a young age, that I really never thought much about the special opportunities that I had been given.

Now, with nothing but time on my hands, I tried to put it all into perspective. I thought about the life that I would be living if I had stayed in teaching. I wouldn't be traveling the world, living in a fabulous apartment, driving a luxury sports car, or wearing designer clothes. On the other hand, who was I traveling with? Who was I wearing the clothes for? And who was I spending time with in my fabulous lake-view condo?

Everyone else who was close to me had a partner. My friend Richard had a partner. My brother was married. My sister had a husband. I had nothing except a bunch of gold and platinum records, and they weren't doing anything for me sitting up on my wall. I had the money to travel, but I had no interest in going alone. While I still occasionally met men in a bar, I never got to know much about them. And those I did get to know a bit better often ended up to be disappointing.

There was one guy I got involved with who turned out to like my Mercedes much more than he liked me. I figured that out pretty quickly. Then there were the cruiser types who had a partner waiting back at home. One night I hooked up with a John Kennedy look-alike who turned out to be of the latter variety. After I realized what was going on, I said, "Listen, it's time to go back to your boyfriend."

I tried to keep a sense of humor, but I began to ask myself more and more frequently, "Life is ticking by . . . who are you going to share this with?"

CHAPTER NINE

AND NOW FOR
THE BAD NEWS

Enter Ron. They say that fate sends you what you need when you really need it most. Perhaps fate was with me the night that I went to see a performance of the Chicago Gay Men's Chorus. The chorus was formed in Chicago in 1983 and was a great organization that not only attracted musically talented men, but also addressed many of the political and social issues of the gay community through song. I wasn't part of the chorus myself. In retrospect it's probably an organization that I should have participated in during the break from Styx. But I did know several friends who were part of the group.

One evening, some of the guys called to invite me to go to see a performance of the chorus. I rarely turned down an opportunity to see the group perform. Any opportunity that allowed me to feel connected to music and to the gay community—even for a few hours—was a great distraction. So I went with a group of friends to the theater.

Afterward, we all met up with some of our mutual friends from the chorus for a drink. On this particular night, there was a new man in our little group of friends who caught my attention immediately. He was extremely attractive; tall, blond, and Southern Baptist. Everything I was not. When I stood next to him, he was about four inches taller than me. I was smitten from the start.

Eventually—fueled by a couple of cocktails—I got the courage to wander up to the small group of men that he was talking with and join the conversation.

"Hi, I'm Chuck." I extended my hand.

"Hi, Chuck. I'm Ron. Nice to meet you," and he shook my hand.

Not to overdramatize the moment, but I felt the positive energy between us right away. There was something about his demeanor—beyond his good looks—that was kind and gentle. I definitely wanted to know more.

Eventually, we broke away from the crowd and began talking alone together. I found out some basics about him. He worked in a professional position at a local department store. He was twenty-nine years old at the time, six years younger than I was. And he lived at Marina City—a Chicago landmark in my neighborhood. That was one of the many things that we had in common. I lived at Harbor Point—a short walk away from his apartment. As we continued talking, we seemed to have a lot of similarities. I liked his sense of humor. He seemed to like mine. And since we were both at the chorus performance, we obviously had a love of music in common.

I was more guarded about revealing too much about myself. When he asked what I did, I told him that I was a musician. He seemed interested, and asked what I played. I told him that I played bass guitar, but that I wasn't with a band at the moment. His interest seemed polite, but not overly concerned. I appreciated the fact that he didn't press the issue. He had no idea who I was or what I did, and he seemed to like me anyway. After being burned by a few gold diggers in the past, I loved this about him. So, breaking my usual pattern, I mustered up the courage to ask him for his phone number. He gave it to me.

When I got home that night, I could not get Ron off my mind. It had been a long time since I had met anyone who had interested me so much. He wasn't someone with whom I wanted to have a quick one-night fling. He was someone that I really wanted to get to know. As I sat in my apartment and the hour got later and later, I had to reprimand myself. I said, "Chuck, are you going to get up the balls to call this guy? If you don't, this opportunity is going to slip away. It'll be, oh well, another train went by."

I picked up the phone and dialed. Ron answered.

"Hello?" He sounded foggy, like he may have been sleeping. It was late.

"Hi. It's Chuck." Pause. "Chuck—from tonight."

"Hi, Chuck." He sounded a bit surprised to hear from me so soon, but not in a bad way. "I'm glad you called."

That's all I needed to hear. We talked into the night and made plans to get together for dinner in a few days. When the time came, we went to a Japanese restaurant in our neighborhood and ended up having a great time. We decided to keep on seeing each other.

Our early get-togethers were the usual first-date-type experiences—movies, dinners, museums, and concerts. He lived about five blocks away from me, so it was very easy to get together for a drink, or to drop by each other's apartment on a moment's notice. Ron and I began to share some wonderful experiences and to spend a lot of time together. Before I knew it, Ron and I were becoming a couple.

The more I got to know about Ron, the more I liked him. He was outgoing in some ways and a bit shy in others. He grew up in Hammond, Indiana, and was from a regular working-class background like me. But his job was taking him all over the world, so he was far from a small-town boy. For his age, he had a very mature outlook on life. His career was very important to him, and he had a good job at Marshall Fields, a top department store just a few city blocks from where we lived.

I suppose I envied him a bit in that regard. Obviously, I wasn't working at the time. I was still having a difficult time dealing with the fact that I was unemployed, and having to tell my story to another person made the glaring difference in our professional lives even more pronounced. At first, I tried not to talk too much about myself. But inevitably, the question of what I did for a living arose. It was a touchy subject for me. I didn't want to bring up my career with Styx, because there was no more Styx. How do you respond to the question, "And what do you do, Chuck?"

"Oh, why I used to be a famous rock musician with one of the highest-selling rock bands of all time. Thanks for asking." It just brings up more issues than it's worth.

Ironically, when I did end up telling Ron about my music career, it was almost a non-event. He never really listened to rock music, so he had no clue about Styx. Weirdly, that really appealed to me. After a wild fifteen-year ride with the group, and the ensuing disappointment and depression over its demise, I was ready for a new life that had little to do with the one I had left behind. With Ron, that's what I got.

Since we lived so close, we would often spend the night at each other's apartment. We even lived together for a period of time while his place was being redone. During the day, Ron would go off to his job. I used to call him "Working Girl" because he was an extremely hard worker. I knew he would go places in his career and become very successful—which he did. During the day, I would hang out and wait for him to come home. In the evenings, it was all very domestic. We would spent time together in my condo, cooking and eating and playing with my cat. I had a fluffy little kitten that Ron loved. In fact, he liked her so much that I bought him a Siamese cat for his birthday. Of course, Siamese is one of the noisiest of all the cat breeds. One day, Ron called me, complaining, "This cat never shuts up!"

I said, "Don't worry. She'll outgrow it."

I later found out that the cat lived to be sixteen years old, screaming the whole way through. If you want to drive someone you're dating crazy for a really long time, buy him a noisy pet. He'll think of you long after you break up.

Ron had a great group of friends who were also in committed relationships, and soon we found ourselves hanging out as a couple. This was the first time that I was ever part of this kind of group, and it was a bit overwhelming. On the one hand, they were all great guys and I enjoyed spending time with them. On the other hand, being with them sometimes emphasized just how different I was from the rest of the group.

When Ron first brought me around, I don't think they quite knew what to make of me. They were all young, professional men, with regular day jobs. And for the most part, they were all very open about their sexuality. Both personally and professionally, they were quite comfortable in their own skin. Many had jobs as designers or other careers where they were around other gay men all the time. Maybe I was a little paranoid, but their day-to-day experiences were so different from mine that I felt like an outsider. As I mentioned before, many gay men at the time had little interest in rock music, and when they found out what I did—or had done—I couldn't help but feel that they looked down on me a bit. If I had been a musician with the symphony—or hell, even a disco queen—that might have been OK. But a rock musician? That made them wary.

Maybe Ron's friends noticed something else about me too that made them wary about my relationship with their friend. Despite the fact that I loved spending time with Ron, I still wasn't completely comfortable with the idea of being part of a gay couple. He had opened up his entire world up to me. But I still couldn't completely let him in to mine. As a result, I wasn't always the most considerate partner. When Ron turned thirty years old, I didn't have a party for him. His friends were surprised and disappointed in me—and they ultimately let me know it. I screwed up. I know I should have done something publicly to celebrate such a big occasion for Ron, but at the time, I simply chose to ignore it.

After only a few months into our relationship, I began to discover just how difficult it is to share your life with another person. At least, it was difficult for me at the time because I had never developed the skill set needed to make this kind of relationship work. I think many gay men are generally less prepared for their first romantic relationship than heterosexuals. We miss all the rites of passage that accompany dating. Your first Valentine's Day card, high school dances, the prom, your first fix-up by your favorite aunt.

If gay boys and girls *do* participate in these events, they are usually forced together with someone of the opposite sex, and the passages become merely societal rituals that teach them nothing of love or relationships. Unfortunately, gay adolescents often spend their formative years going through the motions to become something that deep in their hearts they know they don't want to become. So, all of that is a long way of saying that even though I wanted to have a close relationship with Ron, I was ill-prepared for this type of intimacy. And scared to death.

Until my relationship with Ron, life had always been all about Chuck. I was clearly the center of the universe; my needs, my issues, my codependent relatives. It was all about me. As a result, I was not ready for some of the sacrifices that you have to make in a relationship. If I was in one of my ornery moods, even the pettiest of inconveniences could set me off, causing problems where there were none.

I remember one weekend Ron and I took a trip up to Spring Green, Wisconsin to tour a Frank Lloyd Wright house in the area. I was really looking forward to seeing the house, but once we got to the inn where we were staying, things started to go downhill. Our room didn't have a television, and for some reason, that really annoyed me. I started whining and complaining, which set the mood for the rest of weekend. Clearly, I was grappling with my own intimacy issues that had nothing to do with television. By that night, even *I* couldn't stand being with myself anymore, so I can imagine how Ron felt.

Finally, it hit me. I thought, "What are you doing? You're here with your partner, your buddy. You're spending time together, seeing some really cool stuff, what's wrong with you? You're ruining this."

I knew I had to apologize to Ron for the way that I was acting.

I said, "Ron, I know I've been giving you a hard time. I'm an idiot. I didn't mean to do that."

He had such an understanding demeanor that he was willing to give me a break. We managed to salvage the end of the weekend together.

In the 'Hood . . . John, Emily, Martha, Chuck, and Wayne. About 1952.

Chuck's First
Guitar.

The Original Boy Band: Chuck, John, and Dennis, 1962. *Source: Chuck.*

A Faceoff in
Art School,
Late 1960s.

Opposite:
And Then
There Were
Four, 1968.

John's Wedding:
The Groom and His
Best Man, Early 1970s.

Chuck Spends His First Royalty Check on New Wheels, Mid-1970s.

Hair, Beautiful Hair, Early 1970s.

Relaxing with Richard, Saugatuck, MI, Early 1980s.

A Sweet Hug for Mom, Early 1980s.

. . . As Lieutenant Vanish, 1983. *Source: Michele Morkis.*

The Panozzo Twins, About 1991.

Jan, Joe, and Richard . . . Best Friends in College—and Today, 1997.

Las Vegas, September 11, 1999. *Photos by Susan Turnbow.*

Chuck's return to the stage, Las Vegas, September 11, 1999. *Photo by Susan Turnbow.*

Overcoming the Odds: Las Vegas, September 11, 1999.

Tooling Around
South Beach, 2001.

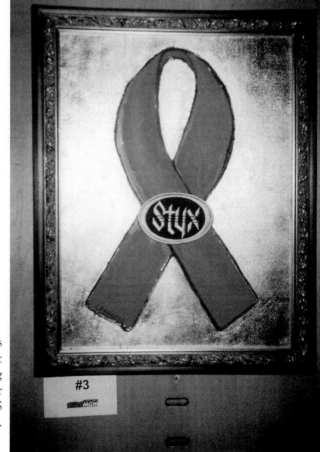

Chuck and Tim's
Painting for Rock Art
Show Benefitting
Elizabeth Glaser
Pediatric AIDS
Foundation, 2001.

Sound Check. *Photo by Jason Powell.*

Backstage. *Photo by Jason Powell.*

Casino Rama, Ontario, November 1, 2003. *Photo by Brigitte Boulais.*

Beacon Theater, New York, June 23, 2004. *Photo by Mark Lew.*

2005 Tour.

Dylan and Chuck ... Two Generations of Rock, 2005.

Chuck's Biggest Fans ... Michele Morkis and Mary Jean Lelek, 2005.

With Tim at the Hard Rock, Hollywood, FL, 2005.

Chuck today. *Photo by Howard Zucker.*

Ron was more experienced than I was about relationships. He had had other relationships with men and wanted to live his life openly. I still didn't have his courage. Ron had moved to Chicago from Hammond, Indiana. Geographically it is not very far from Chicago, but in many respects it is a million miles away. In fact, one day Ron took me there to show me where he grew up and to meet his parents. That was a strange, albeit brief meeting. Ron introduced me as his friend Chuck. His parents were lovely, Southern Baptists, who, I'm guessing, were not big rock fans. I'm certain that to them Styx meant nothing except for the "sticks and stones" variety, and they had no idea who I was or what I did for a living. What they did know was that I was Italian, from Chicago, fairly young to be driving a Mercedes, and seemingly very chummy with their son. They clearly looked horrified. We laughed on the way back home about what his parents thought I did for a living, how they thought I got such a sweet car, and what in the world they imagined I was doing with their son.

Ron had the chance to reinvent himself when he moved to the city, outside the eyes of his relatives and the friends that he had known while growing up. I didn't have the same experience. For me, Chicago was home, and everywhere I went I ran into people who knew my family or me. This made me more cautious than Ron, and more guarded.

One time, Ron and I decided to throw a fundraiser at my apartment for Jane Byrne, the first female mayor of Chicago. She was a progressive candidate who ran on the position of reform. She was also the first mayor of Chicago who recognized the gay community, enacting the initial executive order banning discrimination against gays and lesbians in Chicago city government. We were both big supporters of Ms. Byrne, as were most of our friends.

On the night of the event, we had a great turnout. In addition to many of our joint friends, many of my long-time acquaintances and even my brother and my sister came out to show their support. When Jane Byrne arrived, instead of staying just a few minutes as planned, she ended up spending over two hours at the party. Overall, it was a great success, and I felt good about doing something positive for a candidate who was so supportive of the gay community.

As the night came to a close, I noticed that Ron was sitting alone by the window. I walked over to him, ready to chat about our great success, when I noticed the expression on his face. There was no other word for it—he looked sad.

I said, "Ron, what's wrong?"

He said, "All night you introduced me as your friend Ron. Is that what I am Chuck, your friend?"

He was right. Rather than introducing him as the cohost of the party, or as my partner, I had merely been introducing him as "My friend, Ron," all evening. I hadn't even consciously realized what I was doing, but now it was clear that my internal filtering system had been in high gear. Maybe it was because my sister and brother were there. But either way, I had completely overlooked Ron's feelings. Now, seeing the look of hurt on his face, I felt horrible.

I said, "Ron, I'm so sorry. I just didn't see it."

Ron, being who he was, let it go. But I didn't sleep at all that night. I just kept chastising myself with the thought, "You don't know even what a relationship is . . ."

Obviously, my inability to acknowledge our relationship to the outside world was a source of tension between Ron and me. But despite everything that I did wrong, we managed to stay to together for over a year. Right around that time, my brother started having some problems. His first wife, Debbie, left him, taking their young daughter with her. John was already drinking, which contributed to the breakup. But now that the marriage was crumbling, his drinking was getting out of control. John's life was becoming increasingly desperate. As always, I appointed myself his savior.

Eventually, John moved out of the large house that he owned in the suburbs of Chicago and got an apartment downtown very close to Ron and me. During the day, while Ron and the rest of the world were off at work, I would hang out with John. Also unemployed, John didn't have anywhere to be in the daytime either. We should have formed a club for Unemployed Rock Stars; it would have made a great reality show.

I would usually go to John's apartment around noon to pick him up for lunch. We would go out to a restaurant, order lunch, and inevitably have a few drinks. After we ate, our conversations always went something like this:

Chuck: "Ok, what do you want to do for the rest of the day?"

John: "I don't know."

Chuck: "Want to go shopping?"

John: "I don't feel like shopping."

Chuck: "Want to go to the gym?"

John: "I don't like the gym."

Chuck: "So what do you want to do?"

John: "Let's have another drink."

Most days, we would end of going back to his apartment, where John would continue drinking for the rest of the afternoon. I didn't like this—but there was only so much I could do. I also felt that if he was going to drink himself into oblivion, it was better that I was there with him to make sure that he didn't get into trouble and to try to keep his drinking somewhat limited. I also tried to convince myself that he was only going through a difficult period. I really believed that if I could get him out and involved in life again that he would get his drinking under control.

Ron meanwhile was watching this all from a distance. This allowed him to grasp the situation much more clearly than me. He became very prophetic. One night, when we were alone, he whispered to me, "You know I'm going to lose you, don't you?"

I thought he was crazy. I said, "Ron, what are you talking about?" He said, "John's here now."

I reassured him that my relationship with my brother had nothing to do with us. But, of course, it had everything to with us. As the weeks progressed and John spiraled deeper into his alcoholic depression, I was pulled deeper into his world. All of my emotional energy was going toward by brother, and by the time I would see Ron I had nothing left to give. I knew that this was unfair to Ron, so eventually, I did what I thought was best. I ended our relationship.

I remember the day vividly. It was afternoon, and I simply said, "Ron, this isn't going to work."

He wasn't surprised. After all, he had predicted this. Later that day, I accidentally cut my finger so badly that I knew I needed stitches. I didn't know who to call to help me get to a hospital, so I ended up calling Ron. He should have told me to go jump in lake, but instead, he came over and took care of me. Then he went back home—alone. I simply was never there for Ron the way that he was there for me.

It didn't take me long to realize what a huge mistake I had made. It was only after I lost him that I realized how much I loved and missed Ron. I had let my brother come between me and the man I loved. Of course, it wasn't John's fault. The mistake was mine. I had allowed myself to think that John needed me more than I needed my own life. I was the one who decided to spend more time with John than with Ron. I was afraid to make a full commitment to another human being.

Part of my fear of commitment was that I knew I could not allow Ron into all aspects of my life. I still felt the pressure to keep that part of my life separate from my family. My mother was still a big presence in my life and I could never have brought Ron home to meet her. One time, I remember bringing a casual friend home to meet my mother. After we left, she said to John, "Why did Chuck bring someone gay home?"

John said, "Chuck can bring anyone he wants home." But we all knew that wasn't true.

I don't place all the blame on my mother either, but this kind of pressure is difficult to overcome. I know she was just a product of her upbringing. Many ethnic, immigrant families would have reacted the same way. To save face, parents sometimes ask their children to deny their individuality. And to save face, many children conform. In my own instance, my relationship with my family created a vicious cycle. My ties to my family made it difficult to develop other meaningful relationships. And, since I didn't have other meaningful relationships, my ties to my family were even stronger. I continued to be the perfect codependent son and codependent brother, and in the process I lost someone I loved very much.

Once I realized what I had done, I tried to make amends with Ron. But he was too hurt. Everyone has his limits. Soon after, Ron was offered a job at a prestigious design firm in New York City, and he accepted. We had a few phone calls and correspondences after he left, but eventually it all ended.

I know that I can't blame John, my mother, or anyone except myself for not having the courage to say, "This is who I am," and cultivate a true relationship with Ron. I had never been in love before. It took me a long time to figure out those feelings. Once I did, I had to say, "This is gone. You screwed up." But I don't regret a minute of our time together. Ron taught me a life lesson, something I needed to learn.

After many years, Ron came back into my life. We made a connection when I was playing a concert date in New York. He came to see me with the guy he was dating at the time. They came backstage to see me, and we instantly fell into our old repartee. While his date was out of eyeshot, I pulled him aside and whispered, "This can't be your boyfriend. You're much too good for him." He laughed. A week later, they broke up.

After meeting up again in New York, we kept in touch with phone calls and e-mails. The day the screaming Siamese cat that I had given him died, he called to let me know. It was a sweet gesture. I said, "Ron, I'm very sorry. Tell me, is there enough fur left to make me a toupee?"

To this day we're friends. About four years ago, we actually met up again. Through a friend, he let me know that he was going to be in Miami and asked if I would like to get together. It was a wonderful reunion and we reestablished our friendship. We still have feelings for each other, but now it's more like a brotherly love. Two summers ago, Ron and I, our partners, and a group of friends all went away to Key West together for the week. We had a wonderful time, and I couldn't help but marvel at how far I had come since our days together back in Chicago.

I learned a lot from Ron. The main lesson was, "Get yourself straightened out, or this will continue to happen with other guys. Don't drag anyone else into your little psychodrama." My relationship with Ron marked a major passage in my life. I will always hold a place in my heart for him.

By the end of the 1980s, I had mastered the art of flower arranging, become the self-proclaimed king of adult education in the Greater Chicago area, experienced my first real love, and suffered my first taste of heartache. I was still living in Chicago and had become resigned to a life that was as predictable and tedious as the slow-moving Chicago winters. Can you say clinical depression?

It had been six years since Styx broke up. Since then, Tommy had put out a few solo albums, as had Dennis and JY. None of them had the same success with their solo careers that they achieved with Styx. And while there were periodic rumblings of reuniting during that time, each attempt faded out as quickly as it surfaced. Scheduling issues, and perhaps some unhealed bruises, always kept the band apart. In 1989, the phone calls started again. But this time, miraculously it looked like a reunion might actually happen.

The good news was that four out of the five original members were ready to go. Tommy Shaw, however, who had just joined the rock band Damn Yankees with Ted Nugent and Jack Blades, was not going to be part of the group. This was disappointing, because Tommy's shoes are not easy to fill. But I think we were all eager to get back to work, so we decided to proceed without him.

Dennis called a New Jersey–based musician to fly to Chicago and audition with us. His name was Glen Burtnik. In addition to playing the Asbury Park music scene, including the famed Stone Pony of Springsteen fame, Glen had recorded two albums for A&M in the mid-1980s. When he came to the audition and we all started playing together, the search was over. Glen became the fifth member of Styx, with Tommy's blessing. I wasn't entirely sure how we would sound without Tommy, but we were all anxious to get back to work after so many years. And, at that point, the creative differences between Tommy and Dennis were still so strong that it probably couldn't have happened any other way.

I couldn't wait to get back to work. After a six-year hiatus, I was back to doing what I loved to do best and what felt natural. As a band, it wasn't all love and kisses, but after such a long break, if our temperaments had not exactly turned sunny, at least we had softened around the edges. I was also optimistic that getting back to work might be good for John. In 1990, we went back to the studio to record our fourteenth album, *Edge of the Century*. All was good with the world.

It all started with a cold. We had just started working on the album, and during the long rehearsals I was getting really tired and run-down. I realized that I just wasn't feeling well. I had aches and pains and sniffles—all the symptoms of a nuisance cold—but I couldn't seem to shake it. So I decided to see a doctor near my house. I didn't give much thought to where to go or who to see because I was only really looking for a little reassurance of the "take two aspirin and call me in the morning" variety.

I remember waiting for the doctor in the cold examining room. She came in and routinely did her thing: held down my tongue, looked in my eyes, listened to me breathe. Just as routinely, she popped the question that every gay men dreads, "Would you like to have an HIV test?"

I hadn't been thinking about HIV—I had a cold. But when I heard her question, it all made sense. I can't say that I felt fear—exactly. Things just kind of went into slow motion. I felt like I was watching the whole scene in a movie—and knew how it was going to play out.

I thought, "I'm from that era. How can it not be? What makes me Teflon?" As the script dictated, I said, "Yes. Maybe I should get tested."

In those days, it took several days to get the results back. I drove back to my apartment in a daze, and for the next week went through the motions of my life as if nothing major was happening. I went to rehearsals. I cooked dinner. I watched television. I hung out with my brother and my friend Richard. I didn't tell anybody about the test. When thoughts of the test popped into my mind, I would push them aside, not willing to let myself feel either despair or optimism.

The next week, I drove back to the doctor's office. Again, I was led into the examining room. When the doctor walked into the room, she did not meet my eyes, and mumbled a greeting. She began rifling through her clipboard, lifting the sheets of duplicate form paper. I could feel my heart beat. The room was cold, and I was shivering a bit.

When she began to speak, she said, "Well, Charles, the results of the HIV test were positive. We should test again to assure that this in not a false positive."

I heard the buzz of her monotone voice continue in my ears, but I didn't hear anything after the word "positive." Eventually the buzzing stopped, and I met her eyes.

"What should I do?"

"As I said, we should take another test today to see if the results come back any differently."

"Is that likely?"

"It's procedure."

"So . . . if I am positive?"

"I suppose there's nothing to be done right now. We'll take the other test. We'll see."

I waited for her to continue. She stared back. Finally, she broke the silence.

"It is a serious illness. I'm sure you know that." She straightened up and closed her clipboard, scribbling on the front sheet. I shook my head.

"The nurse will come to take another blood sample." She nodded. I thanked her, and robotically took off my jacket and rolled up my sleeves.

The nurse came in the room a few minutes later. I could tell instantly from his demeanor that he understood my situation. He, unlike the doctor, met my eyes and smiled.

"Hi, I'm Jeff."

I nodded back.

"So I'm going to take some blood."

He felt my arm for the vein. I nodded again.

"How are you feeling?"

"Okay."

"I know how hard it can be waiting for the result. I'm HIV positive myself."

Somehow it was so comforting to know that someone else—even a complete stranger—understood. I asked him the only question I could think of.

"What do I do now?"

"I can't tell you what to do. But for a start, get a flu shot." He added, "You don't want to get any sicker."

So that was the first medical advice that I received in response to my HIV diagnosis—a flu shot. At least it was more than the doctor told me. Dr. Cold Dead-Fish. She had no interest in telling me what to do or where to go. Looking back, I truly don't think she knew what to tell me. She probably saw few cases of AIDS in her small clinic—in fact, I might have been the first one. Her lack of knowledge does not make me angry; her indifference does.

Unfortunately, my experience was not uncommon in those days. In the early 1990s, many doctors were ignorant about HIV protocols and callous toward those infected. In the early 1990s, it was not unusual for newly diagnosed HIV and AIDS patients to be told, "Go home. Get your things in order." This implied, of course, ". . . and wait to die."

Many doctors at that time just didn't want to deal with it. There was a lot of fear surrounding the disease, even in the medical community. No one was 100 percent sure how it was transmitted. It was really necessary to seek out specialists, doctors who studied HIV. Many of the first specialists were gay themselves and committed themselves to finding a cure for the disease that was killing their friends and partners. If I had looked for better medical care at the time, I could have found it. But I wasn't ready. I was still in denial.

Obviously, the second set of test results confirmed the original positive reading. The reality of the situation slowly began to sink in. But I wasn't ready to share my diagnosis with many people. The first person I told was Richard.

Richard's partner, Henry, had passed away of AIDS in the mid-1980s. When he told me at the time that Henry had died, and what he had died of, I didn't have the courage to ask Richard if he had been tested too. Richard was very high-strung, and rather than upset him, I simply kept quiet. But now that I had been tested and diagnosed positive, I found the courage to broach the subject.

I said, "Richard, I've finally been tested. I think you should get a test too. Your partner died—the likelihood of you being exposed is very high."

Richard closed down. He didn't want to hear it. He was more afraid of being "found out" than of the illness itself. He said he was afraid of losing his job. In fact, he was afraid of losing it all. He had bought into the brainwashing that somehow gay men should be ashamed of this illness and ashamed of their life choices. It's amazing how fear and shame can be stronger than the will to live.

Rather than say, "It's better to be alive and shunned by a few closed-minded moralists than dead," Richard, and many others at the time, chose the latter. For some gay men, being tested and found positive was deemed worse than being dead. In either case, they felt their lives were over.

This way of thinking was somewhat understandable considering the way that the AIDS crisis was handled during the 1980s. AIDS was first reported in 1981. Ronald Reagan had recently taken office on a conservative platform that promised, among other things, to consider issues of morality and family in social policy. His election fueled the "New Right" movement in American politics. Some of those who ascended to power in his organization held political and personal beliefs that were hostile toward gay men and lesbians. People with AIDS were often scapegoated and stigmatized. Groups like the Moral Majority blocked AIDS-education programs in schools, and its leader, Jerry Falwell, called AIDS "the wrath of God upon homosexuals."

Meanwhile, William Bennett, the secretary of education, was calling for witch hunts that would require mandatory testing for HIV for foreigners applying for visas, marriage license applicants, hospital patients, and prison inmates. There were even calls for quarantining and tattooing all people with AIDS. Reagan himself avoided any public mention of the AIDS crisis until 1987. Any social and political gains that the gay movement had achieved in the 1960s and 1970s were slipping away. Obviously, all of this served to spread misinformation, fear, and hatred, at a time when information could have saved lives.

The right information was not even filtering down to the gay community—at least not effectively. Even though we knew of the AIDS epidemic and we knew that we should have safe sex, few followed that rule with any discipline. It took a while to sink in. Most gay men in the 1980s had been through the sexual revolution just like the rest of the country, and it was hard to go backward. As the song says, "Those were the days my friend . . ."

The second person after Richard who I told that I was HIV positive was John. It was hard, but in the end I couldn't keep something like that from my brother.

When I told him, his reaction was a slap of reality for me.

I said, "John, I got some bad news a couple of days ago. I went to the doctor and got an HIV test. I came back positive. I'm HIV positive."

John looked concerned. He paused for a while, then he said, "What would people say if they found out that you were HIV positive?" After this kind of reaction from my own brother, I knew that I had to be very careful with whom I shared this information.

I learned that I was HIV positive right at the beginning of rehearsals for the new Styx album. I wondered, "Can I really keep this a secret from the band?" At the time, people were not completely sure how HIV was transmitted. I knew, of course, that it was transmitted through sex and intravenous drugs. There were, however, still a lot of unanswered questions and misinformation circulating. No one really knew if it could be transmitted through open wounds or even by hand shaking or drinking glasses. And since we would spend twelve-hour days together as a band in very close quarters, sharing meals and drinks and bathrooms, I was a little concerned. But in the end, I simply couldn't risk telling them. I had waited for this opportunity too long.

To be safe, I had my own little rituals that I would go through. I always kept my cups and glasses separate and never got too close to anyone. This helped me rationalize my decision to keep silent. Since I wasn't telling the band about my HIV status, I felt obligated to make sure that there was no chance of them catching anything from me (or conversely of me catching any colds or viruses from them). I owed them that much.

I was also playing games in my own head. I tried to convince myself, "You look like the same person. You feel like the same person. You just have a cold. Just go along with the program. It will all be fine."

After receiving the second confirmed positive test results, I did not seek out any additional medical care. In fact, I stayed as far away from doctors as I could for the next few years. I went about fighting the disease in my own way. I started working out religiously and got my body into its best shape in years. Again, I fooled myself into thinking, "If I look this good, and I feel this good, nothing can be that wrong with me."

Part of my reluctance to seek out any treatment was simply denial. But part of my reluctance was also the realization that there were not many treatment options available. The primary drug used to treat HIV/AIDS at the time was AZT, and the side effects were often so bad that death was sometimes a more appealing option. People outside of the gay community who never came face-to-face with the drug probably thought that AZT was a miracle remedy. At least it seemed to offer hope. But those of us inside of the circle who actually saw the horrific effects of this drug had a different view.

One of Richard's friends had been on AZT right around the same time that I was diagnosed. He was a good-looking guy—a big-time player. Richard was visiting him at his apartment one day. They were both out on his balcony. Richard stepped inside for a minute. When he looked back out, his friend was gone. Richard ran outside. To his horror, he saw his friend laying on the pavement five stories below. He had jumped to his death. The drugs were so unbearable that his only out was suicide.

I was terrified to go down that path despite the possible consequences of doing nothing. I decided to wait and to hope for researchers to develop new drugs. I just kept my fingers crossed that I would be on the right side of the bell curve in terms of treatment. It was a gamble with fate, but I didn't see the options.

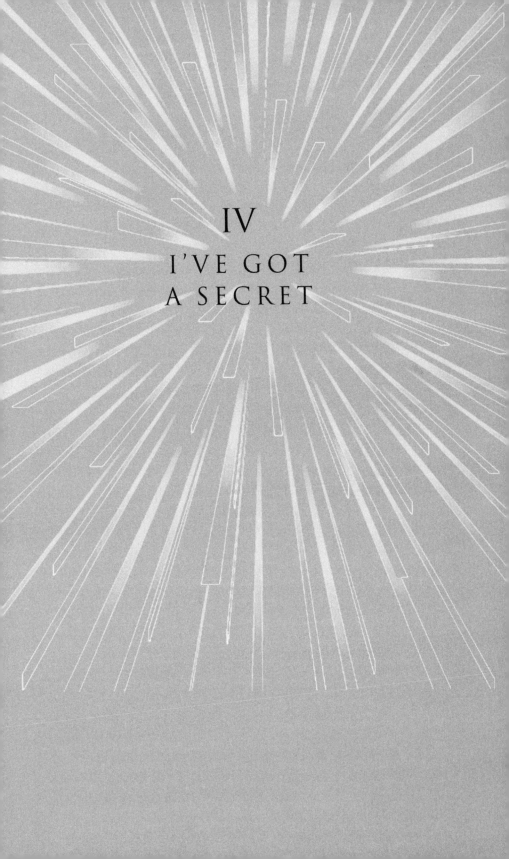

IV

I'VE GOT
A SECRET

CHAPTER TEN

THE WORST
OF TIMES

The early 1990s proved a difficult balancing act for me. I was battling the shame, physical challenges, and depression associated with my newly diagnosed condition, while simultaneously trying to restart my musical career with Styx.

The group was forging ahead without Tommy, and we set out to record our first album of the new decade. During the ensuing years after our breakup, I suppose it had become more obvious to the rest of the group that I was gay. It was never something that I openly talked about, but they weren't stupid. I was in my early forties, never married, never in any relationships with women. After all the time and effort that I had spent trying to hide my sexual orientation in the early years of the band, it had become an unspoken understanding. Time is sometimes the greatest outer of all.

Besides, the world had changed quite a bit since we last worked together. For one thing, gays and lesbians across the country were becoming much more vocal—spurred in a large part by the escalating AIDS crisis. ACT UP—the acronym for AIDS Coalition to Unleash Power—was making headlines in cities across America with its attention-getting demonstrations and acts of civil disobedience. But I quickly learned that inside the band, things hadn't changed very much at all.

One day, it got back to me that one of the band members had

complained to the rest of the group, "I don't mind Chuck being gay. But he isn't going to be one of those Act Up guys, is he?"

That comment hurt me a lot. It told me that the band members were fine with me being gay—as long as I stayed in my wardrobe case. That is, as long as I didn't publicly reveal my pride and allegiance to the gay community. I couldn't help but wonder, "And what if I did? Would you actually put pressure on me to leave the band?"

But, as much as my pride was hurt, I hadn't worked in almost six years. I desperately wanted to get on with my career, and quite honestly, to start putting some more money in the coffer. Also, I was still freaked out by my newly diagnosed HIV status. Honestly, I wanted to keep as low a profile as I could. So I let it go. I said nothing. On the inside, however, I was ashamed that I didn't have the courage to confront the band member who had made this comment and see what he had to say to me. My one solace is that if this were to happen today, I know my response would be very different.

So, I put the remark out of my mind and focused on the album. But there was more trouble ahead. Shortly before we were about to go into the studio to begin recording, I got a call from JY.

"Chuck, we've got to talk about John," he started.

Before he even continued, I knew what he was going to say.

He continued, "Dennis and I talked it over and we both agree. John's drinking has gotten out of control. It's affecting his work. Unless he gets help, we're going to have to replace him on the tour."

I didn't respond.

"Chuck, you know it's the right thing to do. Don't you? We love John, but he needs help." Pause. "We thought you would want to be the one to talk to him."

My initial reaction was anger—how dare the band make this decision about my brother. There would be no Styx without John. And how dare they put the burden of telling him on me. But after thinking it through a bit, my emotions settled down. I knew that they were right. I also knew that if anyone needed to speak to him about it, I wanted it to be me.

John's drinking had been spiraling out of control throughout the 1980s. In the idle years after the breakup of the band, and the breakup of his first marriage, there were few demands for discipline and little routine. For a guy like John, this was a dangerous combination. He always had an addictive personality; that was evident even as child. He was always causing some kind of havoc in our household, at school, everywhere. I would just look at him from a distance and whisper to Emily, "Our brother is crazy, you know that."

Of course, while his antics endeared him to the other kids, our parents and the school's nuns were not amused. In those days, no one understood conditions like attention deficit disorder or other learning disabilities, so John was never given the special attention that he probably needed. Back then, all they did was hit you if you acted up. John got more than his fair share of physical abuse—all for something he probably couldn't control. Unfortunately, as an adult, he sought to comfort his wounded soul in all the wrong places—especially on a bar stool.

Once I admitted that the guys were right in insisting that John get help, I didn't waste anytime in confronting him. He only lived a few blocks away from me. I walked over to his condo, and not surprisingly, he was drinking, but coherent. Although I saw him on a regular basis, for some reason this time I was struck, as if seeing him for the first time, at how frail he looked. He had definitely begun to deteriorate physically. This made what I had to say a little easier.

"John, we all love you, but the band has decided that we can't have someone who finds drinking more important than performing. It's hurting the group. You have to go away to get better, or you won't have a job to come back to."

Those were some of the hardest words I ever had to say, but somehow I managed to get them out. John, true to the pattern of a typical addict, became enraged. After his ranting subsided, he reluctantly agreed to go into a 28-day rehab program down in Florida.

After seeing him go through that experience, all I can say is that I wouldn't wish rehab on anyone. It was a very difficult time for him.

And to top it off, most of the people there are kicking and screaming every step of the way. John seemed to go along with the program while he was there, but you never know what's going on inside someone's brain. It's easy enough to make nice with the doctors while thinking, "Screw you," the whole time. I'm not sure that John was ever able to take responsibility for what was happening to him or to the people who loved him. When you're inside the addiction, it's hard to see the truth.

As part of the four-week treatment, the patient's relatives and significant others are supposed to go to the rehab facility during the last week of treatment to talk about their own role in the patient's addiction. When the facility called me, I told them that I would go. But I told them that my mother was too old to make that kind of trip; she would stay home. My sister and I decided that it wasn't necessary for Emily to go either. The only other person who went down to rehab was the woman who John was dating at the time—Jan. John had met Jan after his divorce. She worked at a bar in our neighborhood, so John obviously spent a lot of time there. Jan was much younger than John and liked to do her share of partying too.

During my visit to John's rehab, I spent the week talking about how I helped John to drink as a codependent person in his life. It was true. I inadvertently had been helping him stay a drunk. It was misguided love. I compare my behavior to a parent who won't say no to a child who wants more candy. If the child wants one or two pieces of candy, you would say sure. But if the child wanted to eat the whole pound, you would say no. With John, nobody ever said no. We tried to pretend that he wasn't really drinking as much as he was and looked the other way. Of course, by saying no, the other person could always say, "Go to hell," but that was his problem. I decided that when we got back to Chicago, I couldn't hang with John anymore unless we were doing productive work. No more afternoons sitting around watching John drink.

When John got out of rehab, the band got back to work. One of the first songs for the album that Dennis presented to the group was a ballad that he was calling, "Roll Me Away." The guys were all singing, "*Roll me away . . . roll me away . . .*" and finally I said, "That doesn't make any sense."

They all looked at me. Having just come back from rehab with John, the new words just came to me. I said, "The song should be 'Show Me the Way.'"

Dennis started singing the new lyric and it just fell into place. "Show Me the Way" was born. On the album, Dennis gave "Special thanks to Chuck" on the song credits. I think most songwriters would have given cowriter status to someone who contributed the main lyric to a song, but that's not the important part. To me, when I hear those words, I always think of John's struggles.

It's funny. When you release a song, you never know what it's going to mean to the people who hear it. So many times fans will come up to us after a show and say, "This or that song saved my life. It's the only thing that helped me get through a terrible period of my life." That's nice to hear, but sometimes surprising. Often the song, in our eyes, has nothing to do with whatever problem they mention. Of course, it's all in the interpretation.

In the case of "Show Me the Way," when the song was actually released, the country's attention was focused on the Persian Gulf War. It was the first war that many younger Americans had ever experienced firsthand. Somehow, "Show Me the Way" seemed to resonate with a nation at war. I think this surprised all of us.

The song became a top-five hit. Some radio stations across the country edited the lyrics to include the voices of children whose parents were deployed to the Middle East. It's ironic, because I am so antiwar, yet the public had somehow found a meaning in my words that I would have never imagined. With two other hits written by our new member Glen, "Love at First Sight" and "Love Is the Ritual," *Edge of the Century* actually hit gold-album status. This meant that Styx had managed to produce a gold album in each of the past three decades.

This feat was even more amazing considering what was going on at our record company at the time. In 1989, A&M records signed Styx on for our comeback tour. In 1990, Polygram bought A&M records from its founders, Herb Alpert and Jerry Moss. Herb and Jerry were two of the most professional and talented men in the business. They had always given Styx great support and they were the ones who wanted us back. After the company was sold, however, the folks at Polygram had other ideas. They weren't interested in promoting a band like Styx. They were interested in attracting the youth market with new bands, not in bringing back a classic rock group to the label.

One day, we were on conference call with the guys from Polygram. The other band members and I were in Los Angeles, and we had the new president of Polygram and some of his cohorts on speakerphone across town. I don't even remember what the meeting was about, but I do remember that after he thought that we had hung up the phone, we heard him saying, "I don't know what you guys are trying to do with Styx. They don't even look like a rock band."

None of us could believe what we had just heard. Here we were about to put out an album, and the head of the record company is clearly not behind us. I thought, "This is Wooden Nickel all over again."

I couldn't believe that after all our years and success in the record business that we were being treated so badly. Obviously, they ended up putting very little promotional dollars behind us. But as always, Styx seemed to persevere despite it all. Our music resonated with the public.

After recording *Edge of the Century*, we geared up for a multi-city tour to promote the album. Once again, Styx hit the road, without Tommy, but with the rest of the brigade intact, including John. I don't know if John was drinking or not at the time. I suspect he was. But he managed to stay sober enough to complete the rest of the tour. On the road, we stopped having any alcohol backstage. The days of always having a barrel of beer on tap were gone. We were all hoping that John's life was getting back on track. Of course, John always had some surprises in store for us.

Throughout the tour, John was continuing to date Jan. She was in her mid-twenties; he was in his mid-forties. I believe she saw what she wanted in John and ignored the rest. She saw John as a rock star—not as the flawed human being that he was. John had a beautiful apartment. He bought her great clothes. He was treating her well and showing her a life she had never known. I suppose you can't fault her for being star struck.

During the tour, John made an announcement that shocked us all. He and Jan were going to get married. And they were going to do it on stage, two days from now. Her friends had suggested it, and they both thought it was a great idea.

The rest of John's family did not share his enthusiasm. For one thing, the counselors at rehab had specifically told him not to marry Jan. There was still too much enabling going on in the relationship, and he was not strong enough stay sober in that kind of relationship. I knew this, so I could not pretend to be happy about the marriage and I told him so.

I said, "John, I'm not against you, but think of what's going to happen when this blows up in your face? Marriage should be something sacred, something spiritual. It's not some kind of stunt for a rock 'n' roll stage."

Of course, John was furious with me and anyone else who questioned his decision. Those who congratulated him, he loved. Those who didn't, he wrote off.

When the night came, Dennis made the announcement during one of our last performances of the tour in Tinley Park, Illinois. He said, "Tonight we have a surprise for you. John Panozzo is going to get married, right here on this stage." Predictably, the audience went crazy. The whole thing is recorded on video. When I watch that tape,

I see myself just standing there in a daze, watching the whole stunt transpire. And this is the story of my brother's second marriage on stage, in front of 20,000 people.

———————

Styx closed out its U.S. tour to somewhat mixed reviews. In all honesty, without Tommy, it was a pretty lackadaisical tour. A&M eventually dropped us, leaving us without a label. And on top of everything else, the fighting that had broken up the band the first time was just as bad this time. Despite all this, at the end of the tour, the guys were still getting together for rehearsals. After a few sessions, I told JY, "Don't call me to get back with the band unless Tommy comes back. It's not worth my time."

I meant that literally. After my diagnosis, my time—whatever I had left of it—had become much too precious to waste appeasing egos and doing mediocre rock shows. So, after our brief reunion, Styx parted ways one more time.

Once again, I was out of work. For the first time since my diagnosis with the HIV virus, I had time on my hands to think about what was happening to me. I find that most people who receive this diagnosis experience two overwhelming emotions: fear and shame. I did too. The fear, of course, was because of the physical challenges of the illness, which back in the early 1990s frequently meant a death sentence. And the shame was because somehow I felt that I had brought the illness on myself. Today, when I speak with anyone who is newly diagnosed as HIV positive, I tell them two things: Get yourself medical treatment as soon as possible, and this is nothing to be ashamed of—this is an illness. It's nondiscriminatory.

I don't know who infected me. Even back then, my feeling was, "Who cares?" It really didn't matter. By dating freely in the 1970s and 1980s, before the gay community even knew that the AIDS epidemic existed, contracting the disease was like a game of roulette. At this point, I didn't want to point a finger; I just wanted to keep from spreading the virus to anyone else.

This rendered my personal life during the 1990s almost nonexistent. I couldn't fathom how or why I would want to expose my status to another person. I knew that if I went to bed with someone who was negative, despite the precautions, there was the possibility of infecting him with an incurable illness. Could I live with that? I know some guys who can, but for me, the answer was no. So I decided to just give my love life a rest.

I still enjoyed being around other gay men. For a while, I continued to go to gay bars and to socialize. I found, however, that often it was like I wasn't even there. I was so consumed with my own thoughts, so consumed with my illness, that I wasn't engaged in life. I was fighting constant depression, and quite honestly, didn't see what I had to live for. But again, my family gave me reason to hang on. They had another job for me.

Shortly after the 1991 Styx tour and his impromptu wedding, John's second marriage hit trouble. Part cause and part effect, his drinking began again, this time even worse than before. I had told Jan early on that she was in way over her head with this relationship, but she didn't want to hear it. Like anyone in love, she only saw the best in John. But as the marriage played itself out, John's troubles became increasingly apparent. By the end, there was nonstop battling. Jan took a job, which fueled John's insecurities and sparked his jealousy. This led to more drinking, which led to more arguing, which led to . . . you get it.

One day I got a call from Jan. She was hysterical.

She told me, "John is out of control. I'm leaving him today. I don't want to be alone with him. You better be here when I tell him or I'm going to call the police."

I called my sister and told her, "She's leaving him. She's going to call the cops if we're not there. We can't humiliate John like that. You've got to come with me."

Emily, who had always tried to stay in the background of John's problems, agreed to meet me at his apartment. When we walked in, the place was a mess. There were clothes and empty dishes and bottles everywhere. John was out of it, and Jan obviously hadn't been pitching in on the home front either.

When John saw us, his mind went immediately back to rehab. He started shouting and walking away from us.

"I'm not going. Just get out of here, I'm not going back," he yelled.

I said, "This is not an intervention, John. That's not why we're here."

He snarled, "What do you want then?"

I saw Jan peeking out from the bedroom. I said, "Come out here, Jan. Tell John why we're here. Tell John what you're going to do today."

Jan walked up to us. She said, "I'm leaving you."

John went crazy. He started crying and saying, "You can't leave me. You can't leave."

It was so sad. He's crying. He's drunk. He's high. She's running around the apartment, grabbing whatever she could get her hands on to take with her. Finally, I couldn't watch it anymore. I said to her, "Please just get out of here. I'll make sure you get back anything of yours that you've left behind."

As she was leaving, I had to ask her, "Why did you wait so long to do this? Why didn't you let us know what was going on a year ago? Maybe then I could have helped him. At least you would have left a whole man, not half a man. Do you think he's a broken toy that I can fix? He's not a toy. He's a human being."

They talk about the need to bottom out in addiction, but that day in John's apartment was more than a wake-up call for him. I think it was the point of no return. Jan called me a few times after that saying, "You have to do something. I'm afraid your brother is going to die."

But there was nothing more that I could do. Finally, I had to say to her, "You know what, this is not my problem anymore. I can't fix it. You helped to create this, now you want me to clean up your mess?" I asked her not to call me again.

I don't know if Jan was calling out of concern or guilt. John was still going around telling everyone that he loved her. He was so out of it at that point. I was seeing first-hand how alcohol kills your brain cells and scrambles your mind. It was sad to watch and hard to believe that John let his life sink to this point. He was a smart man, but in some ways, he was always a wounded soul. He never had much self-esteem. I think that's why he hid behind his humor and practical jokes.

I would never blame my mother for all of John's problems, but I do think mothers are extremely important in the formation of their sons' lives. My own mother never knew how to handle John. So in a sense, she tried to emasculate him. She was always telling him not to run, not to play hockey, not to roughhouse—in short, not to be a normal boy. And because I was the "good boy," who found it easier to follow her rules than John, I think my brother always got the subliminal message that my mother liked me better than him. My mother loved both of us fiercely, but she had no idea how to show it.

After John divorced for the second time, his drinking spiraled out of control. And despite my proclamations to the contrary, I could never turn my back on him. I still saw myself as his protector. Of course, no one can solve an alcoholic's problems except the alcoholic himself, but I could kill myself trying. Besides, I had an ulterior motive. By continually trying to help my brother, I had a legitimate reason to push dealing with my HIV status far down on my to-do list.

I also tried to shield my mother and my sister from the day-to-day of dealing with John's illness. My mother knew that he was sick, but it became increasingly difficult for her to see him in his condition. It upset her. John only lived about a half hour from her house, but he didn't visit her for the last five years of his life. As way of preparation, I remember telling my sister and mother that John was getting sicker, and that one day they might get a call that he had passed away. My mother mentioned this to John on the phone.

John, who knew about my HIV status, spit back, "You're going to get a call that Chuck's dead before me."

My mother, confused, relayed the story back to me.

I said, "Don't worry, Mom. It's just the ranting of an alcoholic."

That comment, however, was telling of the animosity that John felt toward me in the last years of his life. By trying to help him, I was also the only one who tried to make him confront his problems. I was the one who insisted he go to rehab. I was the one who wrestled the keys from his hand. I was the one who honestly discussed his addiction with Jan.

John changed a lot during this period because of the alcohol. As his thinking became more clouded, he started to resent me more and more. As an example of his confused thinking, he started to blame me indirectly for his wife's leaving. Jan's best friend was gay. John believed that her friend had influenced her to leave the marriage. Since her friend was gay, John started to believe that all gay men were bad. Since I was gay, I was bad too. Seeing him turn against me like that was heartbreaking, but in the end, I was one of the only people he had, and I could not turn my back on him.

My brother and I continued on this codependent treadmill for several years, with no discernible progress on either of our parts. Then, in 1995, rumblings of another Styx reunion began to stir. I, for one, was all for it. I welcomed the chance to get back to work and have more to focus on than the failing health of my brother and my mother. I also optimistically believed that once and for all we might just be able to put our differences aside and focus on the music.

In 1995, A&M wanted to release a *Styx Greatest Hits Volume II* album. There was one glitch. RCA would not give the licensing rights to include the song "Lady" on the collection. As one of our most popular songs, leaving the song off a compilation album would have hurt sales. After many phone calls and finagling, a miracle happened. The band—including Tommy Shaw—agreed to reunite to rerecord "Lady" for the greatest hits album.

The recording session went well. It was the first time that Tommy was back with the group, and the vocals sounded great. Maybe the years apart had healed some wounds. We decided to give touring another try to help promote the album.

The band again prepared to take our show on the road for the 1996 tour, *Return to Paradise*. I was thrilled that we were going out on the road again, this time with Tommy Shaw back in the group. Yet, this tour was tinged with sadness right from the start.

As they say, it was like "déjà vu all over again." During one of our rehearsals, after John had left for the night, the rest of the guys pulled me aside and asked to talk to me. Once again, I immediately knew that it was about John. They said that they all loved John and knew what a talented musician he was, but that they didn't want him to go on tour this time. They just didn't think he was able to perform up to par anymore, especially with the physical demands of a fifty-city tour.

My emotions overcame me. I started to cry. John *was* the drums. That's all he knew since he was a child. Now, because of his illness, he was losing his gift. He was losing everything. I couldn't fault the band's decision. It was clear what had to be done. By now, John's appearance was quite shocking. He looked about eighty years old and was barely recognizable. It was evident that going on the road with Styx would have been impossible for him.

That didn't make telling him any easier. It's hard to see someone who is in such desperate shape and deliver even more bad news. This time, I brought in support. JY and Tommy were very supportive. We hired an addiction counselor who Tommy recommended to lead an intervention at John's apartment.

During the session, I told him, "John, you can't come on tour with the band this time. We discussed it, and you just can't handle it. We all want you to stay behind, go to rehab and get better. We need to replace you for now, but when you get better, there will always be a place for you."

By this time, John was more resigned. He didn't put up a fight, but the rage was still in his eyes. That night, he got on a plane to a rehab center in Phoenix. But he resented rehab and he resented me for sending him there. The second time around, we knew right away that rehab failed. As soon as he came out, John went back to drinking. It was like watching a slow suicide. I wanted to do more, but I remember a friend telling me, "You can't rewrite the end of this script." I knew that I finally had to break my ties, but it was very hard to do.

In the band, it was decided that Todd Sucherman would take John's place on the drums. Since we were children I had never played with any other drummer except John. Todd was a great musician, though different than John. Todd was very fast. John was very powerful. I always said Todd plays with lightning and John plays with thunder. That first night on stage at the start of the *Return to Paradise* tour, looking back and seeing a different head sticking out from behind the drums was almost too much to bear. Despite the odds, I hoped that it was only temporary, and that someday John would be back.

In July of 1996, the tour took us to New York City. I have always loved New York and was anxious to go out and enjoy the city. But as usual, the guys were out with their partners and wives, and I was sitting alone in my hotel room. This time, I just didn't feel like going out exploring on my own. I thought, "Screw this," and picked up the phone. I called Richard, my best friend back in Chicago, and said, "I'm in New York. I'm bored stiff—and not in a good way. Get on a plane right now and get out here."

He hemmed and hawed and said, "No, Chuck. I can't."

I said, "I'll buy you the ticket. I'll pay for an adjoining room. Just come."

I hung up and got ready for our gig that evening at Jones Beach, Long Island, about an hour outside the city. On the way out, I made arrangements for Richard, just in case. We played the show, and I got back to the hotel that night around 2 or 3 a.m. When I walked into my room, I noticed the door to the adjoining room was opened. I walked in and looked around. "Richard?" I heard a sound coming from the bathroom. I crept toward the semi-opened door and peaked in. There, in his full glory was Richard, sitting in a bubble bath, sipping a glass of wine.

I said, "Oh, tough trip, huh?" It was one of those moments that I'll never forget—two friends, totally at ease, totally onto each other, sharing a moment of total absurdity. We both cracked up.

The next day we spent the afternoon shopping on Madison Avenue. We hit all the city's landmarks: Calvin Klein, Armani, Gucci. We both took home quite a few shopping bags. I bought myself a new watch. It was a great afternoon.

That night we went out to dinner. During our meal, I took my old Rolex watch from my pocket and said, "Richard, you need a good watch. Take this."

He said, "No, you picked out that watch with John. I remember. I can't take it."

I said, "No, John coerced me to buy this watch. I never really wanted it. Besides, I bought a new watch today and I only have one left arm."

He finally accepted my gift. It really was a great moment. I felt so close to Richard during that trip, almost the way I felt when I was with my own brother, before the alcohol took over his mind. Richard and I went on to enjoy the evening on a hot summer night in the city, visiting a few bars and just enjoying the sights.

When we got back to the hotel, I had a message from my sister. Richard was with me when I returned the call to Emily. I looked at my friend and repeated the words that she had just relayed with shocked disbelief. "John is dead."

I was always sorry that I wasn't with John when he passed away. Fortunately, he was not alone in his final days. A woman who John went to college with and who had become a good friend was living with him as his caretaker. After his divorce, one of John's biggest fears was that he would die in his apartment alone. That never happened. Someone was there to call the ambulance when he collapsed in his apartment.

My sister was the one who was with John at the very end. The hospital called and told her and her husband to come right away. Initially, they thought that John had only fallen. But when they got the hospital, they realized what was happening. When my sister walked into his hospital room, John was hemorrhaging from every pore. The sight terrified Emily. With excessive drinking, a person's esophageal walls can get so thin that it becomes easy for them to burst. John technically died from cirrhosis of the liver and esophageal bleeding. But those of us who loved him knew that John had died of much deeper issues.

I know now that despite his joking, jovial nature, John's spirit was injured. He was a sweet, gentle man who was loved by everybody who met him. Yet, in his last moments on this earth, he didn't feel loved. It's so sad to think about. We're all such fragile souls. Yet I comfort myself with the knowledge that I did everything a brother could do, and more.

In the days and weeks after his death, I heard that some of his friends were asking, "Why didn't his family stop him?"

My question to his friends was, "Why did you drink with him? That certainly didn't help." Sometimes people just don't understand the power of addiction. I did the best I could and as much as I could. You can't tape someone's mouth shut. You can't tie him to a chair to stop him from having a drink. My only comfort in those early days after his death was that he was now finally at peace, drumming somewhere in eternity, creating thunder in the clouds.

There were moments during that first year when I was overcome by grief. We began touring again shortly after John's funeral, so I really never took the time to grieve. One day, the band and I were sitting in an airport, waiting to go someplace or other. One of the guys handed me *Billboard* magazine. He said, "Hey Chuck, look at this."

The group got silent. The book was opened to a page that A&M records had taken out as a tribute to John. It was a picture of a young man, John, sitting behind the drums. In the background, was the shadowy figure of John as an older man, obviously worn by time and the many tribulations that life had handed him.

I lost it. My feelings were still so raw. I hadn't gotten over the fact that John was dead. We all thought he had so much more time. Then, to see him again, so young and full of life, was almost unbearable. I continued on the tour, but it was difficult for a while to be on stage. I kept telling myself, "You have to do this. There is only so much you can boo-hoo, because he's not coming back. The only way you can show your brother respect is to play the best you can on the stage and honor his contribution. He's not here, but you're here for him."

Our final tribute to John was on the final date of the *Return to Paradise* tour—coincidentally the autumnal equinox—at the Rosemont Horizon Arena, now the Allstate Arena, in Chicago. During the last song of the night, the lights dimmed, and a photo of John was projected onto the stage backdrop. Dennis dedicated "Show Me the Way" to John Panozzo. The hometown crowd—who probably loved John more than any other fans—ignited a sea of lighters and candles. I don't think there was a dry eye on stage or off. It was a very touching moment. In death, I hope John finally felt the love that he so desperately sought in life.

After John's death, Todd Sucherman became the permanent drummer for Styx. Despite the loss of John, the band had actually started to regain a sense of stability. The 1996 *Return to Paradise* tour was so successful that we followed it the next year with *The Grand Illusion Anniversary* tour, which was also quite well received.

By the end of the *Grand Illusion* tour, I was exhausted. At first, I thought that it might be the lingering depression from John's death. But as the tour continued, I started to feel more run-down, more hurried all the time. I traveled to each city in a kind of haze, not really sure where I was, but grateful to keep moving. I suppose the idea was to keep running from the reality of my life.

Alas, the tour came to an end, and I was forced to sit still long enough to look at what was going on around me. The view wasn't very good. I was still mourning the loss of my brother. My mother was battling cancer. And now, I was getting sicker by the day. I still wasn't taking any medication for my HIV, and the physical symptoms of my illness were becoming increasingly apparent to everyone but me. It was the end of the tour, and I tried to convince myself that I was simply run down from all the traveling. I still wasn't ready to deal with the reality of my condition.

My mother was dying too. And, my focus, my priority, had become taking care of her despite what was happening to my own body. I moved back into my mother's home and was spending as much time as I could with her. By the summer 1998, I was feeling worse than ever. I had developed a bad respiratory infection and cough. I was weak. I was tired. I was supposed to be taking care of my mother, but in reality, I was probably in worse shape than she was. Slowly, my sister began stepping in to take my place when it simply became physically impossible for me to offer much help to my mother at all. Upon Richard's insistence, I finally allowed him to come and pick me up from my mother's house and take me back to my condo where I could begin to focus on getting better.

Toward the end of the summer, I got a call from our manager. He had some interesting news. Apparently, the members of Styx had been talking, and the group was interested in getting together again to record another album and go on tour. Was I interested? Common sense might have told me that I should have sat this one out, but hey, it might only be the flu, right? So, I said, "*Sign me up.*"

We began recording in the fall of 1998. The studio was a thirty-minute drive from my home, and I struggled to make the sixty-mile trek every day. Inside the studio, conditions weren't much better. The weather outside was turning cold, and despite my heavy winter clothing, I was always freezing. On top of that, every day was a struggle to stay awake. I would doze off whenever we had the slightest break in the action, and I was constantly distracted.

The guys must have noticed how much weight I had lost, but they weren't really focused on me. I heard that one day a recording engineer asked, "Gee, Chuck sure is sleeping a lot during the sessions. Is he okay?"

They said, "Yeah, he's okay." End of story—we have a record to get out. And I felt the same way. I didn't want to make a big deal out of what was happening to my body. I just wanted to focus on making the album.

Secretly, I was anxious to put down my part of the track as fast as possible because deep down I knew that my window might be closing quickly.

At that point, I didn't know quite how serious my condition was, but all the indicators were suggesting that there was something drastically wrong. I began passing out, without warning, on a frequent basis. One day, driving home from the studio, I crashed into a pole pulling into my parking spot. It shook me up, and I called Richard to tell him what had happened.

I was so weak and shaken up, I could barely speak into the phone. While Richard had gamely played along with my denial for many months, he could take no more. He said, "Chuck, get your things ready. I'm coming to get you. I'm taking you to the doctor."

When Richard came to door, I could see the look of shock in his eyes. It had been a while since I had seen him, and the changes in my appearance were occurring rapidly. Red spots—Kaposi's sarcoma—had begun to appear on my body and my weight had dropped to 130 pounds. My clothes were falling off my emaciated body. I just shook my head.

I said, "I know, Richard. It's time. We'll find a doctor."

I had been so ashamed to get help for my problem. I was so ashamed to tell people what I had. But finally, I had to ask myself the question, "Do you want to live, or do you want to die?"

Obviously, when I look back, I realize that I just wasn't ready to accept the fact that I was so sick. I tricked myself into trying to beat it "just one more day." Of course, every day that I stalled was one more day closer to dying. It would not have been the HIV that killed me, it would have been one of the complications of the disease—and I was getting all of them: Kaposi's sarcoma, anemia, and thrush. They were about to overwhelm me.

I was diagnosed with AIDS in late 1998. This time, the physician I visited was an expert in treating AIDS and HIV-related illnesses. He practiced at the NorthStar Medical Center in Chicago, which was run by a visionary physician who was one of the first to use protease inhibitor therapy to fight the HIV virus.

After Richard brought me to the clinic, I was advised to start treatment right after the holidays. The doctor was prescribing a very aggressive, 23-pill per day regimen. As soon as I began treatment, the side effects of the drugs knocked me out, and it was only a sheer will to live that kept me swallowing the medicine every day. At first, I almost gave up. I gave the doctor a very hard time, taking out my anger at both the disease and the treatment on him.

Finally, I had a realization. I said, "Are you crazy? This guy is offering you an opportunity to live. Don't pass that up, because no one else is doing that right now." So I shut up and kept swallowing.

Shortly after I began my treatment in January, my mother Betty took a turn for the worse. But the meds were making me so sick that I couldn't be with her as often as I would have liked. This was heartbreaking for me, because I had been there for her my entire life. And even more heartbreaking, I still didn't feel that I could tell her the real reason that I wasn't by her side. My sister began taking on the full brunt of my mother's care. Since she was giving up so much of her time to be with my mother, I knew that I owed Emily an explanation. On one of the last visits to my mother's house, I sat Emily down.

"Emily, I've been to see a doctor, and they know the reason that I'm not feeling well. It's not a cold or a virus. I have AIDS."

Emily said, "Oh, don't worry, Chuck. I'm sure in a couple of years you'll just be able to take a pill for that. You'll be fine."

This is the same sister who told me I was going through a phase when I told her I was gay at twenty-one. Obviously, denial dies hard.

I can't say that I wasn't hurt by her initial reaction. I thought, "Don't you even care? I'm dying." But I know that Emily cared deeply. She had just been through too much. Her mother was dying and she had just seen her other brother destroy himself. I remember seeing Emily when I came back to Chicago after John passed away. Her eyes were like slits. I said, "Emily, what's wrong?"

She said, "I can't get any sleep. Every time I close my eyes I see John in that hospital bed. It's just too much."

Emily was watching everyone close to her slip away, and she simply couldn't bear the thought of losing me too. I came to understand that, so I tried to shield both her and my mother from my illness. I would check in by phone, but there was no need to upset them by making them witness the slow deterioration of my body.

When my mother would ask Emily where I was, my sister would simply tell her that I wasn't feeling well. After my mother went into the hospital in her final days, I knew that I couldn't stay away any longer. I had to say good-bye. Standing at her bedside along with some other visitors, I overhead my Aunt Terese say, "Betty looks bad, but Chuck looks worse."

At the same time, I was also still trying to put my best face on for the band. We had been together recording for a few months when we agreed to play at a PBS convention in Chicago. Although I was feeling extremely weak that day, as was the norm at the time, I went to the gig. I wasn't going to let the guys down. At the end of the set, the mixer signaled to me that he couldn't hear me. I was confused at first, and checked my connections. Everything seemed OK. I tried it again.

He shook his head. After a few more attempts, I realized what we happening. My fingers were simply too weak to hit the strings hard enough. One of the producers came up to me afterward. She looked very concerned and asked softly, "Chuck, are you okay?"

I said simply, "I'm okay," and walked away.

That night, the band hung around a bit longer than usual. They were milling around as if they had something to say, but their eyes quickly averted mine when I looked at anyone. Finally, Tommy Shaw held my gaze. I knew that they wanted an explanation. I knew that was my opening. But I wasn't ready. I said, "Good night," and left the building.

Shortly afterward, I got an e-mail from Tommy asking something along the lines of "Come on, Chuck. We know you're gay. We know about HIV. Is that what's going on?"

It wasn't a hostile e-mail. It was more of a, "Hey, we can't ignore the white elephant in the corner anymore. It's standing on its head and playing the trumpet."

I knew it was time to be honest with them. The next time we were together, I told them that I wanted to tell them all something. I said simply, "I've been to see a doctor, and I've been diagnosed with AIDS."

After watching my body wither away for the past several months, I don't think they were shocked, but I'm sure it's always unsettling to hear those words.

"I've started treatment and I need to take it one day at time. I can't tell you with any certainty when, or if, I'll regain my full strength, but the band is still very important to me. So if I can be with you, I will be." I wanted them to know that I wasn't throwing in the towel yet.

I really didn't know how they would take the news. In general, their reaction was very supportive. Dennis and Suzanne were very kind. Tommy and JY, who I was closest to in the band, were probably the most affected by the news. I know they were also very shaken by John's death, so I'm sure that they were thinking, "First John, now Chuck too?"

During the next days and weeks, I tried to keep going as best as possible, showing up for rehearsals and not dozing off on the job. But we soon discovered that I wasn't the only member of the band who was having problems. Dennis was becoming more and more sensitive to light. He was traveling from doctor to doctor, but no one could figure out what was wrong with him. Apparently, he was eventually diagnosed with a type of chronic fatigue syndrome that caused extreme sensitivity to light. I would never minimize someone else's health issues. But the strangeness of this ailment, coupled with the mounting creative tensions within the group, was putting increased strain on the band. Quite honestly, where Dennis's illness was concerned, I think most of the guys just didn't understand it. Nonetheless, our recording sessions were delayed, so I started out 1999 waiting to lay down my track on the album and getting used to my new life on twenty-three pills a day. Happy New Year, indeed.

CHAPTER ELEVEN

HIV AIN'T
FOR SISSIES

The year 1999 was a difficult one. In January, my mother lost her battle with cancer and passed away. I was reeling not only from the loss of my mother but also from the extreme nausea and malaise caused by my drug treatment. I was living in my Chicago condominium with sweeping views of Lake Michigan. My days consisted of walking from my bed to my recliner. I would sit in my chair, gaze out at the water and enjoy the sunlight that would spill through a wall of windows. I thank God for that apartment, because on most days those views were my only connection to the world around me.

Because of Dennis's medical problems—and the ensuing frustration within the band—our recording of the *Brave New World* album had been delayed throughout the Christmas holidays. By the time we were ready to lay down my track in late January, I was too ill to go back to work. This really upset me. You would think as sick and grieving as I was that I would have just said "Screw it," but I really wanted to finish the album. Deep down, I thought it might be my last.

Tommy and JY understood. They told me not to worry, that I was part of Styx. They said that I had contributed creatively, and my name would be on the album along with the rest of the band. Apparently, not everyone agreed. About a week later, I got a call form JY saying, "Chuck—I've got some bad news. Dennis doesn't want to put your name on the album since you didn't actually play on the final cut."

I said, "Pick me up tomorrow. We're laying my track."

He asked, "Are you sure Chuck? We'll fight to get you on anyway."

I said, "I don't want to be put on the album gratuitously. I want to lay the track."

He was hesitant. "Are you sure you can do this Chuck?"

I told him, "If I can't make it through, you can take me back home. But I've got to try."

The next day, JY picked me and took me to the studio. There was no one there except JY and a few sound engineers. They made sure that it wasn't a big circus. I don't know how I did it, but I laid the track for several songs. I did it for John. I did it for my mother. I did it for myself. And, miraculously, it sounded pretty good. When the other guys heard what I did, the calls of congratulations started coming in. Tommy called. Our manager called. Some of the guys from the crew called.

I got calls from so many people, including JY, Tommy, our tour manager George, and even many of the crew. In the end, I felt very proud of what I had done. I think that being a true man means living up to your responsibilities. While struggling to save my life, I still managed to attend every rehearsal and ultimately to finish the album. I felt very good about that. It was also good to know that after all the years that we spent together, Tommy and JY and George genuinely cared. Even today, the guys look out for me. It's not uncommon for someone to ask if they can carry a bag or get me something to drink. When you see the smiles exchanged up on stage, it's not just an act. They are real.

With *Brave New World* wrapped up, I was free to focus entirely on my treatment. Despite the horrible side effects of the medicines, my doctor assured me that the drugs were making a difference. I was under the care of Dr. Matt (as I'll refer to him)—a twenty-nine-year-old, handsome young doctor right out of medical school. I'm not sure what I was expecting when I first went to see him, but his youthful good looks surprised me. Dr. Matt told me that he had seen me perform in St. Louis. He was a Styx fan. I really wasn't expecting that (a) he would be so young, or that (b) he would know who I was—but I thought, "Okay, Chuck, go with the flow. You really don't have many options here."

Dr. Matt was honest. He told me right from the start, "I can help you with your HIV, but your complications are going to be hard for you." That's why I always tell people to get tested sooner rather than later. It's the complications of HIV that can kill you.

When I first visited Dr. Matt, my viral count was 800,000. In just two weeks, it had dropped to 300,000. When he told me the news, he said, "My God, look at these numbers."

Drawing upon my limited math skills, I shouted, "Wow, it dropped almost 20 percent!"

He smiled back, "No, Chuck, it went down a lot more than that."

I shrugged, "Gee, I guess that's why I play the bass."

Seeing those viral counts drop so suddenly made me fully realize the power of the drug. It was exactly the boost to my spirit that I needed at the time. I knew that if I kept up the treatment, I just might get through this thing alive. So every week I would diligently go to see Dr. Matt. Despite how bad I felt, before every visit I would shower and shave and change my clothes. My friend Richard teased me about this without fail.

"It's a doctor's appointment, Chuck, not a date," he'd say.

But I didn't care. I would tell him, "I haven't thrown in the towel yet, Richard. I still want to look good."

Dr. Matt and I had great rapport. He told me I was one of his favorite patients.

I said, "I guess that means I'm following my protocol?"

He said, "Yes. And you're my most entertaining one too."

My weekly doctor visits were the only time that I would venture out of the house. The outside world had become too perilous of a place for someone as weak as I was. Even the simplest shopping trip could become a hazard. One time, I tried to go into a store and came face-to-face with a revolving door. As I gingerly stepped into the circular entrance, some Type-A came bounding through the door so quickly that I was nearly knocked over. That put an end to my midday shopping expeditions. Fortunately, my buddy Richard was always there to help. He would drive me where I needed to go at off hours so that we could avoid the crowds.

I was also aware of the stares that I got whenever I went out in public. At first, I couldn't figure out why people were looking at me. As I became more aware of my changing appearance, eventually I started to wear heavy clothing to add bulk to my shrinking frame. I tried to hide my body the best that I could, but I still think that people could guess what was happening to me, especially in a big city like Chicago. When I look back at photos, I can see that my face was extremely drawn and wasted.

In the early stages of my treatment, I was also battling one of the common complications of AIDS, Kaposi's sarcoma—the red cancerous spots that eat away at your skin. A biopsy showed that the cancer had not entered my organs yet, but it was on its way. I had spots, which they call strawberries, all over my body. The doctor would freeze off each lesion, leaving behind a scab. Frequently, the scabs would break causing "streamers" of blood that would soak through whatever clothing I was wearing. It was hard to go out in public because you never knew when a streamer might break. Obviously, this curtailed a lot of my life for almost a year.

Fortunately, most of the lesions were on my back and other parts of my body where I could hide them with clothing. But one day, I noticed a lesion on my neck that I could not cover up. I had never had a strawberry on my face, but this one was a little too close for comfort. It totally freaked me out. I went to the doctor and had it frozen off. But at that point, I knew that psychologically I couldn't handle this on my own anymore. There was too much going on with my body and my appearance that was completely out of control, and I needed help. I found it in a stairwell.

During one of my doctor's visits at the medical center, I was walking down the stairs and quite literally bumped into a psychologist who

I'll call Dr. Greg. I recognized him immediately. However, when I knew him, he was Greg, the waiter at the Hamburger Hut where John used to hang out. We always used to joke around together—John even prodded me to ask him out a few times. But I remember responding that I couldn't ask out our boy-toy waiter—it would be a scandal! Well, here he was, all grown up, with a doctorate in psychology.

We chatted for a while, and I instantly felt that he was sent back into my life for a reason. He asked me if I would feel uncomfortable with him being my therapist since we knew each other from our old neighborhood. I said, "No. You knew my past, you know my present, and now you'll know my future."

This decision transformed my life. I do not know how I would have ever gotten through my illness without Dr. Greg's help. I urge anyone who is diagnosed with HIV or AIDS to get psychological help. Talk to a trained professional. Talk to other people who are positive. There is so much to deal with; you can't do it alone.

I think almost anyone who is battling HIV goes through at least a brief period of depression. I certainly know that I did. In addition to battling your own feelings of guilt and fear, the pure physical challenges that you go through are daunting. I was taking about thirty pills a day, and each time I took my medication, I would have to lie down for several hours. Add it up—that's a lot of time on the couch. I was also getting frequent skin infections, which I treated with another assortment of creams and potions. And with a compromised immune system, I was susceptible to all kinds of secondary complications, which were treated with even more medicine.

The changes in my appearance were another source of psychological stress. Each time I looked in the mirror, I saw something different. My body image changed so many times, I didn't know who I was anymore. Initially, AIDS wasting syndrome caused me to lose over 10 percent of my body weight, accompanied by chronic diarrhea and weakness. All of a sudden, your body takes up a fraction of the space that it used to. Then came the drugs. Protease inhibitors tend to cause a distended stomach, yet your cheeks remain sunken and your arms and legs are like little twigs—like a child's stick-figure drawing. The first time you catch sight of this image in the mirror, it really messes with your self-esteem.

At a certain point, I was so starved for physical contact that I would have massages just so that I could feel the human touch. These masseuses were the only human beings that I would allow to see my naked frame. I started to jokingly call myself Dorian Grey. On the inside though, I wasn't finding the humor in the situation at all. I sunk deeper into my cocoon, only seeing a handful of people on a regular basis—Dr. Matt, Dr. Greg, and my friend Richard.

I realize now how wrong it was to cut myself off from the people around me who were trying to help. The only way to make it through any kind of serious illness is with the support of your friends and loved ones. But because of the nature of my illness, I was still ridden with guilt. I couldn't shake the notion that somehow I brought this on myself. I couldn't shake the repeated thoughts in my head that asked, "How could you have caught this thing? How could you have allowed this to happen?"

I did a disservice to myself and to the people who loved me by underestimating their compassion. It was arrogance. I could not believe that their love was stronger than my sense of guilt and fear. Fortunately, many wonderful people in my life persevered despite my insistence to stay away. In the end, they saved my life, and I thank them. If an illness can ever have any positive ramifications, one of them is surely finding out how many people out there care about you.

One of the first people to call me after my illness was Donna. This was Donna whom I had hurt so many years ago by telling her that I could not marry her. A few years before I became so ill, Donna had come back into my life. Her husband had recently died, and she contacted me. She had a son from that marriage, and she still lived in Chicago. It was wonderful to hear her voice on the phone. Some people just seem to have a connection right to your soul, and no matter how much time goes by, the connection is never broken.

We decided to meet. Before long, we were falling into an easy pattern similar to the way we were almost twenty years earlier. I would take her to brunch and lunch, and we ended up spending a lot of time together. Ultimately, I realized that it was happening all over again. I said to her, "Donna, we can't do this. I can't hurt you like this again. You have to get out there. Meet other men. Find a father for your son." So once again, we went our separate ways.

Several years went by. Then, Donna heard through my one of my aunts that I was ill. She came to see me immediately. I was amazed at the generosity and love of this woman. Despite our breakup years earlier, a rift that could have permanently embittered a lesser woman, Donna has remained a dear friend in my life to this day.

My family also tried to reach out to me during my illness. Although at this point I had told very few people in my extended family specifically what was wrong, they knew that I was seriously ill. They may have even surmised the real cause of my illness, but we never spoke about it.

Growing up, my family had been very close with my Uncle Chuck, his wife, Aunt Terese, and their children. During my illness, my Aunt Terese and my cousin Mary Jo would send cards and call often to check in on me. We would talk about how I was feeling in general terms, and they would always ask if they could do anything for me or come to visit. I always politely declined their offers to help. One day, I suppose they had had enough of my protestations.

My Aunt Terese asked, "Chuck, are you eating right?"

In an Italian family you don't answer "no" to this question. I said, "Oh, yes, I'm eating. I'm fine." But Aunt Terese was having none of it. She said, "Chuck, we're coming over. We'll be there tomorrow."

The next day, Aunt Terese, my cousin Mary Jo, and her little daughter showed up at my apartment building with about twenty coolers packed with Italian food. I remember my little cousin was terrified by the doorman, so when I got to the lobby, there was quite a scene of crying and loading boxes into the elevator and shouting. The South Side of Chicago had come to Lakeshore Drive. I felt right at home.

Inside my condo, my aunt and cousin proceeded to put out a huge spread of pasta and meatballs and soup. I ate heartily—a rare occurrence in those days. What we didn't eat, they packed up and put in my freezer. Their goal was to fatten me up. We had a wonderful afternoon. I still remember their visit as one of the kindest acts I've ever known. I don't know why I tried to hide from them for so long, but fortunately they didn't take no for an answer.

Another family member I relied on heavily during my recovery was my cousin Gene. Gene was a hockey nut. When John was alive, the three of us would often go to Blackhawk games together. John was a hockey fan too, and I enjoyed spending time with him and Gene at the games.

Shortly after John died, Gene and his wife Trish had a baby daughter, M.K. We had known Trish's family forever. One day I got a phone call from Gene. I congratulated him on the baby, and then he surprised me.

He said, "Chuck, Trish and I want to ask you something. Would you be the godfather of our daughter?"

I was taken aback. I answered right away, "Of course, I will. I would be honored."

As soon as I hung up, I began to have second thoughts. Gene and Trish didn't know that they had just asked a gay man to be the godfather of their new daughter. I didn't know how they would feel about that if they knew. After all, the christening would be taking place in the Catholic Church, which renounced my sexual orientation. As the godfather, I would be swearing to bring up the child in the tradition of the Catholic faith. I would be taking part in a sacrament under somewhat false pretenses. But even more than that, I didn't know how Gene and Trish would feel on a personal level about their daughter having a gay godfather. After grappling with these issues, I decided not to say anything, and to accept this honor.

On the day of the christening, I brought Gene a hockey jersey that John used to wear—one of his favorites from a famous Canadian hockey player. I think it was special for Gene. When he was only twenty-one, he had lost a brother to brain cancer. Ever since I lost John, we had a special bond with each other.

The ceremony was very nice. During a Catholic christening ceremony, one of the godparents holds the baby over a marble pedestal while the priest pours a little drizzle of holy water over her forehead. While I was maneuvering the baby into position, I thought, "Between the priest and me, we're going to drown this baby. We don't know anything about holding infants." But my goddaughter was beautiful and, miraculously, she survived her christening anointment unscathed.

Gene and I kept in regular contact until I got sick. After I started treatment, he continued to call me to go to hockey games, or just to get together, but I would always make excuses. I could tell that he was hurt. And I suppose that because I felt a special bond with him, I wanted to tell him the truth.

Finally, I worked up the courage to call him. I said, "Gene, I have something to tell you. You know that I haven't been feeling well. What I haven't told you is that I have full-blown AIDS."

Gene was incredible. He said, "Chuckie, I'll do anything that I can to help. Trish and I are there for you."

Of course, that led to the next obvious issue. I said, "I don't know how you and Trish feel about me being openly gay. M.K. is still young. If you don't want to tell her that I'm her godfather, I understand. You can tell her it's someone else."

He said, "You've got to be kidding. We love you and we couldn't think of anyone else who we would want to be her godfather."

Gene and Trish proceeded to learn everything that they could about HIV. They read books and watched PBS specials on the disease. No one could have asked for a more supportive response from two people. They were totally nonjudgmental.

During the winter months after I started my treatment, sometimes I didn't know if I could make it through another night alone. I would take my drugs in the evening, and it would be pure hell for the rest of the night. I would sometimes call Gene to come over and sit with me. He never said no. It was so comforting to have him with me, and to know that he and Trish were there for me. Again, if anything good can come out of illness, it's this kind of unconditional love.

The months ticked by, and I slowly began to regain my energy. I stuck to my drug regimen religiously despite many days when I didn't think I could take anymore. I looked to the two public figures that I knew were bravely battling—and beating—HIV at the time, Magic Johnson and Greg Louganis. I thought if they can do it, I can do it too. Having role models and knowing that I was not alone was tremendously helpful to me. That is one of the main reasons that I was motivated to write this book—to help others as others have helped me.

By the end of the summer in 1999, a miraculous thing happened. I was recovering. When I started my treatment, Dr. Matt told me it would take about two years for me to fully recover my strength. It had shocked me to hear someone say, "Just hang in there. You'll feel better in about two years." In the world of immediate gratification that we live in, that is almost incomprehensible.

But here I was, ten months later, not feeling so bad. As usual, my mind started wandering back to the band. In the spring, while I had been consumed with my own battles, they had been going through a little drama of their own. After the release of *Brave New World*, our record label and the guys themselves were anxious to start touring to promote the album. Dennis, however, was still saying that he was not well enough to perform. Again, his symptoms were vague, and by now Tommy and JY had run out of patience with him. The ongoing creative differences between Dennis on one side and JY and Tommy on the other didn't help resolve matters. The band eventually told Dennis, "We're going on tour, and you're welcome to come or not."

I'm not sure Dennis could believe that Styx would be able to go on tour without him. But it happened. The promoters—believing in the draw of the Styx name with or without one of our members—started booking us.

At the same time, JY made a public statement, saying, "Dennis was going off in a very unilateral sort of way, where it's his way or the highway. We chose the highway."

Of course, I was hearing about all of this secondhand. As much as I cared about the band, when you're faced with a life-or-death illness, everything else seems not quite as important. Besides, even though I supported the group's decision to go on tour, I felt that I should lie low on the issue since I would not be participating.

Lawrence Gowan—a great performer with a strong theatrical voice perfectly suited to our music—was hired to replace Dennis, and the re-formulated Styx started playing concerts. In addition to the absence of Dennis, this was the first tour that Styx had ever done without at least one Panozzo brother on board. The original boy band was MIA. I felt bad, but hoped that one day soon I would be able to return to the stage.

During one of my doctor's visits in late summer, I broached the subject of going back to work. I said, "You know, Doctor, I'm feeling stronger. And there's all this stuff going on with the band. They're on tour. We have a new lead singer. Glen is playing my role on bass. I feel like I'm being left out. I was wondering, what if I did just one show?"

He said, "I realize that you're under a lot of pressure, Chuck. I understand why you want to do this. But I've seen too many guys go back to work too soon. I'm not going to tell you not to do it, but I can't say that I'm crazy about the idea."

I really respected Dr. Matt's opinion, and his halfhearted endorsement worried me. But that's where good rationalization skills come in so handy. I thought, no problem, if it's too much, I can always get on a plane and come back home.

So, despite the odds, on September 11, 1999, I returned to the stage. I chose Las Vegas to make my comeback performance with Styx. I figured if it was good enough for Elvis, it was good enough for me.

Styx had booked two dates in Las Vegas—September 10th and 11th. I wasn't sure if I had the stamina to do both shows, so the first night I sat on the sidelines and watched. I also needed the time to transition back into this world. My life had been so far removed from the music business over the past several months, I wasn't sure I could picture myself back up there on stage—part of a band that now included only two of our original five members and was barely recognizable to me. As I continued watching, I came to realize that I was simply battling fear. If I had come this far, I owed it to myself to get back in the ring.

By the next night, I was ready. As I stood in the wings, I heard Tommy's voice introduce me, "Tonight, we have a special guest artist performing with us . . . also known as the original bass player and cofounder of Styx . . . Chuck Panozzo."

Before he was even through speaking, the fans saw me walking on stage and starting chanting, "*Chuck, Chuck, Chuck!*" The greatest part about it was the joy on everyone's face to see me back on stage.

I'm sure that the crowd was a bit startled by my appearance. I was still very thin and looked quite different than the last time I had appeared in public. No one knew the real reason that I had left the band. At my request, the band's official public relations stance on my absence had been left vague. But my appearance gave away part of the secret. Later on, I heard that after Lawrence met me for the first time in Vegas he said, "God, I'm afraid this guy isn't going to be around too much longer."

Looking back, from a purely physical standpoint, I probably went out too soon. But psychologically, it was exactly what I needed. The fans' response said, "We don't care what you have, we're just so happy that you're here performing in front of us." They made me realize that I hadn't screwed myself out of a job. That I hadn't screwed up so much that I couldn't go back.

Going on stage that evening was an unforgettable, spiritual moment that symbolized so much more for me than returning to the band. I had been on the brink of death and was given another chance. This time around, I felt that I had to give something back. My best friend Richard was about to help me figure out what that was.

CHAPTER TWELVE

A MESSAGE
FROM A FRIEND

Richard was one of the first guys I met when I moved into downtown Chicago in the early 1980s. We hit it off instantly. We were close in age with similar backgrounds. Richard had also been raised with a healthy dose of Catholic guilt. He, however, was served his plate of neuroses southern-style, hailing from Corpus Christi, Texas. I always joked that he looked no more like a Texan than I did—and nobody ever mistook me for a Texan. His family's roots were Basque French, so he had a swarthy, dark complexion.

As I mentioned earlier, Richard's partner had died in the 1980s from AIDS. Despite this, Richard never got tested. When I was diagnosed in 1991, I urged Richard to get a test too. I said, "Richard, we can't hide from this anymore—you need to know." But he always had an excuse. He told me that he didn't have any insurance at the time, so he was going to wait.

I said, "Richard, you may die. Doesn't that concern you?"

But he countered, "Well, you've been diagnosed, and you're still not getting treatment. So what's the difference?"

He had a point. I was not on meds at the time because I was too confused. I saw people on the early AZT regimes who seemed to be getting worse, not better. My thinking at the time was to hope that AIDS drugs improved, and that I would be at the right end of the bell curve. I now see the error in my thinking. I waited so long to begin treatment that I almost didn't make it. But at the time, Richard's logic seemed valid—so I didn't push the matter.

Richard was very much like me—strong-willed and opinionated. But I think his fears about revealing himself as gay went a little bit deeper, and I could never quite understand why. He used to say that he worried about the impact on his career, yet he worked in design. You can't say every designer is gay, but let's face it: You do meet a lot of gay men and women in that industry. Richard's fear that he might lose his job or his status never made much sense to me. I now know that Richard's issues with self-esteem and self-loathing ran much deeper than I ever knew.

Ironically, just after I began my drug treatment and actually began to see an improvement in my condition, Richard's health began to decline. Like me, he downplayed the symptoms. But in January 2000, he took a turn for the worse. Just as my friend had done for me, it was my turn to sit Richard down and make him face reality. I went to his home and said simply, "Richard, it's time."

At first he resisted, but ultimately, he knew he could no longer hide from his illness. In a reversal of roles, I drove him to the hospital where he began his final struggle with this insidious illness. He could barely walk to the car. I knew exactly what he was going through. This was one bonding experience that I could have lived without, but you deal with what life hands you.

The hospital was very close to where I lived in northwest Chicago. I could actually walk there. So for the next few months, I visited almost every day. Richard didn't want me to tell our friends that he was sick, and he didn't want anyone else to see him in his current condition. He had a private room, and other than me, I don't think he had any other visitors except a few elderly aunts whom I never met.

Each time I would leave his room, I would think, "This man is going to go insane. What must be going through his mind right now?"

At this point, the doctors at the hospital had tested him for the HIV virus and were treating him for AIDS and its related complications. Yet, Richard still was not able to share this diagnosis with anyone. He could not verbalize it to me, his best friend in the world, who was also battling the virus. Instead, Richard focused on the tumor on his liver that he was being treated for, as if that was his only concern. It was heartbreaking to me that Richard felt so much shame that he still could not be truthful with me, or with himself, even as he lay dying.

One day, the doctor stopped me when I came outside of Richard's room. He said, "Are you Richard's partner?"

I said, "No, his friend."

The doctor said, "Richard isn't taking this seriously. I'm not sure he understands the gravity of his condition."

I said, "I know, doctor. I'll try to talk to him."

The next day, I gently tried to shake Richard into reality. I spoke softly. "Richard, we both knew that this might happen one day, right?"

His eyes started to tear. He stopped me immediately. "Let's not talk about this now."

I said no more. I didn't want to put any more burden or guilt on him. He was dealing with too much already. Every day there seemed to be another tube inserted into him. Once a football player, he was now skin and bones, and barely recognizable. His handsome face was sunken and pale. And what's worse, he just didn't see this coming. Like me, he stupidly believed that somehow he would escape this disease, even though the odds were against us. We were both gay men of a certain generation who had lived and loved during a dangerous time in our history—a time when the magnitude of the danger was not yet understood. And we were paying the consequences.

After a couple of months in the hospital, Richard had tumors breaking out all over his body. He began chemotherapy and was placed in an isolated room because he was so susceptible to germs. At that point, I had to cut back on my visits. I didn't want to be a carrier to Richard. I was also still quite susceptible to germs myself and was beginning to worry about spending so much time in the hospital environment.

Now that I was feeling physically stronger, I started thinking about doing a few more concert dates with the band. I wanted to get back to work, but I worried about leaving Richard. One day I asked him how he would feel about me going on the road for a bit. Styx was booked for an appearance on the *Today Show* in New York, and I was thinking about joining them.

Richard said, "Go, go. I'll watch you on TV." So I did.

I called Richard as soon as it was over, and of course, he had been watching. He told me that we sounded great and that I looked good on camera. It felt good to know that he had been watching.

In time, Richard was well enough to leave the hospital. He went to stay at an aunt's house. I continued to perform a few more dates with the band in various cities. After returning from one of these road trips, I called Richard's aunt to see how he was doing. The conversation went something like this:

"Hello, is Richard able to come the phone?"

"Who is calling please?"

"This is his friend, Chuck."

There was a pause.

"Richard isn't here. He got a high fever and had to go back to the hospital. He passed away earlier this week."

I was unable to speak. She continued.

"Richard was taken back home to Texas and cremated."

I was still trying to comprehend what she was saying. The silence was clearly unsettling her, so she grasped for conversation.

"How long did you know, Richard?"

"About twenty years."

There was an awkward pause. "Oh, okay. Well, good bye."

I stopped her. "Wait, will there be a memorial service?"

"I . . . I'm not sure. Nothing's been decided yet."

I knew there would be no memorial service. But I didn't want the conversation to end like that. I needed more. Something.

"I know Richard's friends will want to send their condolences.

Can I forward the cards somewhere?" I asked, searching for some kind of closure.

"That won't be necessary," she said. "Thank you. Good bye."

And with that, Richard's life was neatly closed. The family had quietly shut the door on their son so that he could bring them no more shame in death than he had in life. To the best of my knowledge, Richard's mother came to visit her dying son one time while he was in the hospital. Although I never spoke to the woman, I am sure that she stayed away in part because of the shame she felt over the way her son was dying. During his life, he never told his mother he was gay, just as I never discussed it with my mother. As I mentioned, I never met Richard's mother, but I believe her feelings were similar to my own mother's.

In my mother's eyes, admitting that her son was gay would have meant admitting that she was a failure as a mother. In truth, her only failure was not accepting her son and all his complexities. I know that she loved me intensely, but when it came time to talk openly about my life, she would end the start of any conversation in anger. She would simply close down the door of communication. I also know that Richard's mother no doubt loved him just as deeply, and I know that her grief upon his death must have been difficult. But this time, my compassion for Richard surpassed any feelings of sympathy for those who were unable or unwilling to fully accept this wonderful man.

For weeks after Richard's death, thoughts ran rampant through my mind. How did Richard fall through the cracks? What stopped him from walking into a doctor's office for all those years? How strong was his fear of being exposed that he was willing to sacrifice his life to protect his secret?

They say timing is everything. The day after Richard died I was scheduled to record an interview for a VH1 *Behind the Music* special that the network was doing on Styx. I knew that this was great public-ity for the band and would expose our music to an entirely new, younger fan base. My mind, however, was in an entirely different uni-verse. If I had been thinking clearer, I probably would have cancelled, but at the time the option of picking up the phone and telling them that I couldn't make it never ever crossed my mind.

So, I kept the interview. I numbly went through the motions of showering, dressing, and driving myself to the studio to be interviewed. My heart was breaking over Richard, but here I was—camera-ready. When I look back on the interview, I appear so somber. I supposed everyone just thought, "Oh, that's just Chuck. He's always low-key."

The interviewer was asking questions about all the bickering that had gone on with the band—the catfights between Dennis and Tommy, the breakups, the reunions, the jealousy and in-fighting. It was nothing I hadn't lived through already, but hearing it in capsule form was revealing. With every question, all I could think was, "These idiots!" Here was a group of guys with everything going for them— money, health, youth—and they had wasted so many years getting upset about such foolishness. At that point, I knew that I wasn't going to waste any more of my own time.

Richard's death signaled a turning point in my life. I came to real-ize that if you have a brother, you're lucky. If you have a twin brother, you're really lucky. If you have a friend who you would pick as a brother, you're the luckiest of all. I was unable to save my twin brother from addiction. I was unable to save my chosen brother from the shame that ultimately killed him. But I vowed at that point that I would never again allow anyone else to fall through the cracks if I had the power to save him or her.

And I did have power. I had the power to spread the word about AIDS education. I had the power to say, "Please get an HIV test if you think you've been exposed to AIDS. Don't think you're impervious to this, because thousands of others like you thought that they were impervious and they're dead now."

I had the power to live a proud, purposeful, truthful life . . . to live by example. Finally, after fifty-two years, I was ready to live a completely open, honest life. My music—and subsequent life in the public eye—gave me a platform to reach thousands of people. Rather than hide in the shadows for fear of exposure as I had done my entire life, I was ready to step into the spotlight. I did not yet know how or when, but I had a renewed sense of purpose as I planned my coming out strategy.

In the meantime, as they say, shit kept happening. For one thing, I was hit by a car. For another, I got sued. They were unrelated events, but both were a pain in the ass—in one case, quite literally.

Late one rainy night I was crossing the street after stopping to get a quick bite to eat. Here's how I remember it: headlights, screeching brakes, and a stabbing pain in my knee. The next thing I remember was seeing a cabdriver get out of his car and run to my side. He proceeded to yell at me for stepping in front of his cab, got back in his car, and drove away. I felt like I had been pummeled as I lay on the pavement. Eventually, I knew that if I didn't get out of the street, I would end up tomorrow's roadkill, so I dragged myself to my car and miraculously drove myself home.

The next week, while I was still home recovering from the accident, I got an early morning call from my friend Michael. I was still moving very slowly, so I couldn't get to the phone on time. I heard his cheery message playing over the answering machine instead.

"Hey, Chuck. Sorry to call so early. Guess what? You've just been sued, man."

He got my attention. I called him back.

"What did you just say?"

He said, "Get the paper. You're being sued."

I said, "Get the paper? I can't walk twenty feet—what's going on?"

"Dennis is suing you," he told me. "He's suing the band."

Dennis DeYoung had filed a federal lawsuit claiming misuse of the Styx trademark. Everyone in the band found out the same way. We called each other almost simultaneously, asking, "Did you see the paper? Can you believe this?"

The article in the *Chicago Sun-Times* went like this:

For more than a year, the rock band Styx has been on the road without its co-founder, Dennis DeYoung. And he wants that to stop. DeYoung went to court Tuesday in hopes of preventing the band from "damaging this beautiful thing that we created."

The group's former lead singer filed a lawsuit in federal court claiming misuse of the Styx trademark by former bandmates Tommy Shaw, James Young and Charles Panozzo.

"This is the most painful decision of my professional career," said DeYoung, who helped found the band 35 years ago in Chicago, wrote and sang most of the group's hits, including "Lady," "Come Sail Away," "Babe," and "The Best of Times."

DeYoung, who lives in the south suburbs, said a partnership contract renewed in 1990 by him, Shaw, Young, Panozzo and Panozzo's brother John, required the agreement of all five on all matters concerning the band and the Styx trademark. John Panozzo died in 1996.

"Now they have taken the band's name and excluded me from the decision-making process," said DeYoung, whose vision brought Styx much of its success. "I have asked for a meeting since July of 1998, and the response I've gotten is that there is no interest in talking."

DeYoung joined Styx on a successful reunion tour in 1997. When the band was planning to hit the road again in summer 1999, he asked to delay the tour because he was suffering side effects of chronic fatigue syndrome. The other members refused and went ahead without him. DeYoung is seeking unspecified monetary damages, including a share of the profits from the tour and recovery of his costs and attorney's fees.

Shaw and Young, the only original members on the current Styx tour, were performing in Canada on Tuesday and had no comment. "No one within the Styx organization knows anything about a lawsuit filed by Dennis DeYoung," manager Charlie Brusco said.

Conflict between DeYoung and his bandmates is nothing new. Other Styx members disliked wearing flamboyant costumes and speaking in grandiose dialogue in the 1983 tour DeYoung spearheaded for the conceptual album *"Kilroy Was Here"*. *The band seldom played together for the rest of the decade. In a new episode of "Behind the Music" receiving heavy play on VH1, Shaw and Young mock and ridicule some of DeYoung's musical concepts.*

Concentrating on theatrical work in recent years, DeYoung recorded an album called "Ten on Broadway," and his stage musical "The Hunchback of Notre Dame" was produced at the Tennessee Performing Arts Center.

Young told the Chicago Sun-Times *in June that the decision to tour was a case of "majority rules" egged on by a dislike for the musical direction that DeYoung preferred.*

"The majority made a decision in 1999 to go on without Dennis— Tommy Shaw and myself and Chuck Panozzo, even though Chuck is on a leave of absence," he said. "Dennis's priorities have not been directed toward the band. The theater thing—he's just going off creatively in a dramatically different direction than what the band is about in my judgment, and he's going off in a very unilateral sort of way, where it's his way or the highway. We chose the highway."

DeYoung hopes to work things out with the band. His health has improved and he is touring with an orchestra, performing new versions of Styx songs. "I have said from the beginning that reconciliation is absolutely the way to go," he said. "I'm still hoping that there will be a happy ending to all this."

The happy ending never came. In fact, after that day, I never saw Dennis again. Dennis wanted to conquer the world on his terms. If anyone else had an idea or an opposing view, he didn't want to hear it. It's undeniable that when we were together with Dennis in the 1980s, Styx was at its best. It would have been great if we could have all worked together again, but the psychological angst that went along with that was more than any of us could bear at this stage of our lives. Ultimately, this would bring more harmony and artistic freedom to the band. It was a turning point in our professional lives, and if it brought with it some ugliness, so be it.

For me, I simply could not bear wasting anymore time bickering over trivial matters. And after what I had just been through, it was all trivial. I wanted to play music and touch people's hearts. I wanted to lead a happy, productive life. I wanted to focus on what really mattered. I wanted to make a difference in the world. It was time to end the bullshit and to start living a more genuine life.

I was finally ready to begin my journey as an openly gay man.

CHAPTER THIRTEEN

WILL THE REAL CHUCK
PLEASE STAND UP

I came out almost a year to the day after Richard's death, on July 28th, 2001, at a Human Rights Campaign dinner in front of 1,000 friends, family members, and strangers.

One thing that I tell people as they make the decision to come out is that if you are not comfortable with going public, then wait. Coming out is not obligatory; it is an option. I am especially concerned about young people. If publicly declaring that you are gay is going to get you abused or kicked out of the house, then don't do it until you are old enough to live on your own. The streets are ugly, and the last thing you want to do is end up getting into drugs or prostitution.

At a certain point, however, most people are going to want to come out. You start feeling better about yourself. It's a monkey off your back to say, "I want to live my life as an openly gay person."

Once you say that, it's like the key to open the magic box. It frees you to be a better thinker. Suddenly, it doesn't matter if someone says that you look or talk like a faggot. Instead of freaking out, you have the courage to answer back, "You can't say that to me. I'm not going to allow you to say that to me." It's an empowering feeling.

After Richard's death, I knew that I wanted to live my life as an openly gay man and that I wanted to help others struggling with this same issue. I also wanted to come out in a very public way—to make a definitive statement that I was no longer willing to hide my sexuality from anyone—fans, family, friends, even the inevitable bigots. I no longer cared who knew. In fact, I wanted everyone to know.

I started telling my friends what I had in mind. Their reactions varied. One friend said, "Yeah, right. You'll never do it."

Another said, "Right, Chuck. You're just doing it to get laid." I was insulted, but considered the source. Both of these men were still living in a sexual limbo—out when convenient, but with a firm hand on the closet door.

Some of my most positive encouragement came when I was visiting Florida in January 2001. Styx was invited to play the pregame for Super Bowl XXXV in Tampa. It was a fun time, playing in front of 72,000 people along with Ray Charles, The Backstreet Boys, and Sting. After the gig, I went to visit some friends in Miami.

I was always interested and supportive of the Gay Men's Chorus in Chicago—especially after meeting Ron there. It had a special place in my heart. And through that organization, I had met some members of the Miami Gay Men's Chorus as well. During my visit to Miami, one of my friends in the chorus invited me to one of their practices. I went, and after rehearsal, I decided to test the water a bit. I made an announcement to the group:

"Thank you for having me. Participating in a group like this is very meaningful to me. I am in the early stages of coming out, and the example that you all set is inspiring."

There was a roar of applause. I was moved beyond words. I knew that I was preaching to the choir—pardon the pun—but I thought that if these people were so supportive, maybe others would be too. Their excitement was contagious. These men were living what I was still only dreaming, and having their support gave me the courage to take the next step.

From that point on, I knew that my public outing was really going to happen. It was only a matter of time. Coming out became one of my primary goals and I wanted it done. When my brother died, someone else wrote his obituary—someone who did not know him and did not know what he was all about. When Richard died, he didn't even get an obituary. When I died, I wanted my obituary to say more than, "He died of complications from HIV." I wanted people to know my story, and the only way that this would happen is if I told it while I was still alive. So I went about knocking on doors, trying to find the best platform for my coming-out debut.

Through my research, I learned about a wonderful organization called the Human Rights Campaign Foundation (HRC). This group has helped countless gays and lesbians find the courage to live a more authentic life. The primary goal of the HRC is to ensure basic human rights for the gay, lesbian, bisexual, and transgender community. As an advocacy group, they do great work lobbying Congress, supporting fair-minded candidates, and educating the public on a wide range of issues important to the lives of the GLBT community. The HRC also offers support to anyone who needs help with the coming-out process. For anyone struggling with this issue, I urge you to visit the HRC website at www.hrc.org. After my first meeting with the Chicago chapter of the HRC, I knew I had found my forum.

———————

I told them my story and that I wanted to come out in a public way in order to help others who might be struggling. I told them that I would like their help and guidance. We came up with an idea. With their encouragement, I made plans to come out at their annual dinner in my hometown of Chicago in July.

Once I knew that this was really going to happen, I started calling the important people in my life. One of the most difficult phone calls was to my Aunt Terese, who was something of a surrogate mother to me. Aunt Terese was in her seventies, a religious woman, who probably had little or no exposure to anyone gay in her entire life. Yet, when I told her what I planned to do, she was completely supportive. It was touching to me that this woman who had lived a life steeped in decidedly antigay, Catholic, Italian-American values was able to accept me and love me for who I was. I'm sure it wasn't easy, but she opened her mind and opened her heart. My aunt's acceptance, perhaps because she was like an extension of my mother, meant so much to me and helped to heal a part of me that had been hurting for so long.

Hers was the first of many surprisingly positive responses when I began to share my plans with friends and relatives. Aunt Terese's husband, Uncle Charles, and her daughter Mary Jo were equally supportive. So were my sister, her husband Bob, and a brood of California cousins who wrote me, "Chuck, we've always been proud of you, but every time you do something else, we just beam more with pride."

I also called each member of the band and told him my plans. The one conversation that I remember vividly is my call to Tommy Shaw, who was living in Los Angeles. He said, "Well, Chuck, you know what this means. Now you'll have to move out to West Hollywood, too." I had to laugh.

Reactions like this were comforting to me. I began to realize that once again, I had underestimated many of the people I loved. I had projected my own preconceived judgments upon them, assuming that they would somehow look down upon my sexual orientation. It was confirmation that as ugly as people can be sometimes, they can also surprise you for the better. I also came to realize that some people in my life would simply never be able to accept or understand my sexual orientation. I didn't waste my time trying to change their minds. You can't crack every nut, and that's okay. I think it's important for anyone just coming out to realize this and move on.

Springtime passed quickly, and before I knew it, the HRC dinner was right around the corner. In the weeks leading up to the event, I was a bit nervous, but mostly excited about the turn that my life was about to take. As I invited my personal guests to the event, I was touched by everyone's support and eagerness to attend. During those weeks prior to the event, I also spent a lot of time thinking about and writing my speech. It took me a while to define the role that I wanted to play in the "human rights campaign" of life. I didn't want to come out for my benefit only; I wanted to come out for the benefit of the entire GLBT community. In fact, I wanted to come out for anyone who ever felt discriminated against because he or she was different. This larger statement of inclusiveness became my platform.

Finally, the big night arrived. It was a lovely Chicago evening. As I stood outside the hotel, watching the well-dressed crowd arrive for the gala, flashbacks of my life flooded my mind. I knew that life as I had known it would soon be over. At fifty-three years old, I was about to be reborn.

Inside the banquet room, it was the usual cacophony of clinking glasses, muffled conversations, harried waiters, and air-kissing heads. I took my seat, and I'm sure that I made the appropriate small talk, but inside I was a million miles away. At my table, I had my sister and brother-in-law, my aunt and uncle, my cousin Mary Jo, Dr. Greg, and my friend Michael. Other acquaintances were scattered throughout the audience, as well as several supporters who had recently come out publicly. JY—who I named an honorary gay guy that night—was there to represent the band.

Finally, the moment came to take the stage. I walked through the crowd with all eyes upon me. Looking out from the podium, I wasn't exactly nervous—it was all too surreal. I was watching myself in a slow-motion movie, and I couldn't wait to hear what I was going to say next.

I remember saying these words: "I have been in the closet for so many years. It's time to step off the shore and plunge into the lake . . . I've lived in Chicago my entire life. But being here tonight, speaking to my gay brothers and sisters about coming out, means that I am finally home. I want to live my life as an openly gay man." Saying those words changed my life.

The rest of the night was a blur. I was walking on a cloud. I remember piling into a limousine with Michael and a few other friends. There was quite a bit of champagne involved, which led to a bunch of grown men hitting each other over the head with throw pillows in the back of the car, and probably at least one instance of poking our heads out of the sunroof—but I digress. When we got to my house, the gang wanted to come up and continue the party, but I said, "No, no, no . . . you're already hitting each other with pillows. That's enough for me tonight."

In truth, I needed a moment alone to reflect on what had just happened. The best way that I can describe the feeling was a tremendous sense of relief. Coming out freed my soul and set my spirit free. I was soaring. Of all the rituals that I had been through in my life—communion, confirmation—none of which I understood very well, the ritual that I had gone through tonight at age fifty-three was the most meaningful. Before that evening, I was angry all the time. I was angry at life. When I accepted myself, I accepted the world, and my anger faded. I felt a little guilty that it had taken me so long to get there, but in the end, the only thing that mattered was that I had made the journey.

———————

The next day, the congratulations started pouring in from friends and acquaintances all across the country. Some of the comments were funny. One guy I had known a long time called me and said, "You know, I always knew you were gay."

I said, "You work in a gay bar. You used to serve me drinks. Of course you know I'm gay."

As the event and news of my coming out spread through the press, I began to receive more support and words of encouragement from all over the globe. Styx had been quite popular overseas, but I never could have imagined the number of letters and e-mails that I received from other countries. It was particularly touching to hear from young people who said that I had helped them accept who they truly were. For me, that's what it was all about.

One of the fans who sent me an e-mail following the HRC dinner was a young woman named Michele Shnell. She wrote me a beautiful note expressing her support and asking if I had thought of doing a website to share my story. In fact, she volunteered to set it up for me. I was touched and accepted her offer. That site became an important vehicle for me to reach out to fans and anyone who might find comfort in my story and my words.

In addition to reaching out to people on my website, I began to do speaking engagements across the Midwest. I was particularly interested in speaking to young people who were struggling with the issue of being gay. Having known the pain and loneliness of growing up different, I was eager to begin speaking to youth groups. Ideally, all children would grow up in loving, supporting homes that nurtured and accepted each one's individuality. Unfortunately, that doesn't always happen. Children can't choose their parents, just as I don't believe they can choose their sexual orientation.

One of my first speaking engagements was at a summer camp in Peoria, Illinois for gay and lesbian teenagers. I must admit that I was a little nervous at first. I was used to performing in front of thousands of people, but this was the first time I was "performing," so to speak, on my own merit. As soon as I met the kids, though, my fears melted. We had a wonderful conversation, shared lots of hugs, and took lots of photos. I told them how proud I was of them. It takes a lot of courage to admit to your feelings at that age, especially growing up in farm country where most of them lived. I told them that I grew up in a city, and I still faced prejudice and ignorance throughout my youth.

I also talked to them about responsibility. Of course, practicing safe sex and getting tested regularly was part of it. But I also asked, "What are you going to do once you pass the fun part of your life—the dancing and the dating? There is still so much work to be done on behalf of the gay community. We're still practicing unsafe sex. AIDS is still ravaging the world to little attention. Our own country still does not give equal rights to gay partners. What is your contribution going to be? How are you going to help?"

I hope that this made them think about their responsibility. Not everyone has to grow up to be a gay activist, but everyone can think about what their contribution will be to making the world a better, more tolerant place. I still keep in touch with some of the kids that I met at these speaking engagements. Almost always, I am moved by the courage and character that these young people are showing as they move on into the adult world. In some small way, I hope that my words helped them in their journey.

By 2002, life was going well. I was busy speaking to youth groups, doing newspaper and magazine interviews, and appearing on radio talk shows. Now that I was out, my life was blossoming and I never felt more fulfilled. A few months into the year, I received another honor of a lifetime. I was asked to be Grand Marshal of Chicago's 33rd annual Pride Parade.

If you've never been Grand Marshal of a parade, I highly recommend it. On June 30th, 2002, as I led the procession sitting up on the backseat of a 1965 Bentley, waving to the 350,000 supporters who had gathered that day, I couldn't help but think of how far I had come in just a year. For the first time in my life, I was living honestly. Leading that parade through my hometown, expressing my pride in such a colorful way, was one of the highlights of my life.

And make no mistake—I was quite colorful. My friend Michael threw a little party for me before that parade and we all got dressed at his house. Some of my oldest friends in the world were there. I looked around at the bunch—most of us were shirtless, with plastic beads draped over our heads and lots of leather. Gay anyone?

I said, "How did this happen? In high school, none of us would even say the word gay, now we're personifying it!" I was proud of how far we all had come.

Throughout the procession, the paradegoers lining the streets could not have been more supportive. Many were screaming, "Go, Chuck! We love you!" or "We love Styx!"

As we approached the end of the parade route, I was still waving to the crowd, when I glimpsed a group of men and women with bullhorns huddling toward the right side of the car. Before I had a chance to process who they might be, I heard their screams.

"Chuck Panozzo, you're going to burn in hell! Burn in hell! Burn in hell!"

Their words stabbed at me. The hatred in their eyes was frightening. I was momentarily confused. I didn't know these people. Why were they spewing such hatred at me?

"You're a sinner! Burn in hell!"

It hit me with a jolt. They hate you because you're gay. It took a moment, but I regrouped.

My self-dialogue went something like this: "What are you freaking out about? Tens of thousands of people turned out today to support you. This has been one of the greatest days of your life. Are you going to let a few assholes with bullhorns take that away from you?"

With that, I sat up straight, turned to face the supporters who were still lining the left side of the street, and gave them my best royal wave. The screams from behind me seemed to fade away. I simply couldn't hear anything they had to say anymore.

As we drove away, I said gently, "Don't worry about my afterlife; worry about your own."

A few years earlier, I would have been devastated by the screams of the protesters. But things were going too well for me to let a small setback get me down. In fact, things were rocking. Literally. The Human

Rights Campaign asked me to be spokesperson for the 2002 National Coming Out Day. National Coming Out Day is celebrated every October 11th to mark the anniversary of the 1987 march on Washington, D.C., for gay and lesbian equality. The theme that year was "Coming Out Rocks," celebrating openly gay, lesbian, bisexual, and transgender musicians.

As a working musician, participating in this project was doubly rewarding. Ironically, rock 'n' roll remains extremely homophobic. So many musicians are gay, but there is still the pressure to hide it. Particularly among male performers, I think there is the perception that if they do not fulfill the rock-stud machismo image, they won't sell as many records. I'm not sure if that's true or not. I'd like to think that the music-buying public is more evolved. I do know that many more female rockers than male rockers are out, and they seem to be doing fine.

For the "Coming Out Rocks" campaign, nineteen openly gay musicians signed their names to a theme poster with the tag line, "You may feel like just a face in the crowd, but coming out as gay, lesbian, bisexual, or transgender makes you a star."

Many gay artists agreed to lend their support to the HRC campaign. Some of the musicians participating included Melissa Etheridge, k.d. lang, Ani DiFranco, Michael Stipe, the Indigo Girls, Janis Ian, and Pet Shop Boys. As a kid who once felt isolated and freakish, you have to admit, I was now part of one damn cool group.

V.

ILLUSIONS
SHATTERED

CHAPTER FOURTEEN

READY FOR LOVE

In 2002, despite all the good things that were happening in my life, I was still struggling with some unresolved issues. In a period of two years, I had lost three people close to me—my brother, my mother, and Richard. Wherever I went in Chicago, I could hardly walk down the street or go into a restaurant where I wouldn't think of Richard or John and suddenly become flooded with feelings of sadness. It was beginning to paralyze me.

Also, Chicago's winters seemed to become more bone-chilling for me each year. And there were too many people. I constantly worried that I was going to get knocked over by the crowds because I was still so thin. Even the simple things like shopping were hard. Every revolving door was a potential hazard. People would spin you around too quickly. I would wait until everyone cleared away from the entrance before going in a store to get my things.

I had a friend at the time named Craig, who lived in Florida. I was talking to him on the phone one day and told him what I was going through. He said, "Come down to Miami. It's the best place in the world. You can reinvent yourself."

Something about the idea appealed to me instantly. I remembered Miami from performing at the Super Bowl with the band. While the thought of living there had never occurred to me, I considered it now. Great weather, a slower-paced lifestyle, no memories—it sounded pretty good. It was February in Chicago and I love the beach, so I thought, "Why not?" Somehow, I felt that even though coming out had changed my life dramatically for the better, my journey was just beginning. I needed a fresh start in a new city. There was nothing holding me in the city any longer. Miami, here I come.

It all happened so fast. I put my condo on the market. Within a week, a couple came to take a look at it and made an offer immediately. I must admit, the place was stunning because I had just renovated the whole thing. As they were walking through the apartment, they were asking, "Oh, can we buy this, can we buy that?"

I was thinking, "Don't you have your own taste and your own stuff? You know how long it took me to find all this?" Maybe my testy attitude was the first sign that this wasn't going to go as smoothly as I imagined.

When I got to Miami, I promptly decided that I had made the worst decision of my life. I hadn't counted on being homesick. The Miami scene was dramatically different from Chicago, my home of over fifty years, and I was feeling culture shock. I didn't relate to anyone. To make things worse, the woman who bought my apartment wrote me a note saying, "Oh Chuck, your place is still so beautiful. We love it here! We're going to treat it very well."

I was thinking, "There's somebody living in my house and they're not going anywhere any time soon. This isn't fair!"

Back in Miami, I was struggling with the adjustment. I didn't know many people. And to make things worse, I had a couple of medical problems, including a skin infection, which forced me to fly back to Chicago for treatment, making a smooth transition even harder. In time though, with the help of a therapist who helped me get my feelings of depression and anxiety under control, I began to feel more at home in Florida.

I forced myself to get moving with my life. I reminded myself that part of the reason that I moved to Miami was to get a fresh start. One of the areas that I was ready to explore was the possibility of forming a relationship with another man. I was eager to have someone to share things with, and, as they say, "the goods weren't getting any fresher on the shelf!" I put the word out to my friends.

Fortunately, gay men love a good fix-up. Cliff, a friend of Craig's, told me that he knew someone he thought I should meet. He invited me to see a performance of the Florida Gay Men's Chorus and also invited a man named Tim. It's amazing how music plays a role in every important moment in my life. He told me that Tim was a painter and that he was also HIV positive. That was actually one of the reasons that Craig had chosen Tim as the "fix up." He knew that I didn't feel comfortable going out with anyone who wasn't HIV positive. I simply didn't want to run the risk of infecting anyone. He didn't tell me what kind of painter Tim was—Van Gogh kind of painter or house painter? But I didn't care—I was game.

Through a series of mix-ups, Tim and I did not actually get to sit together, but we did manage to meet up after the show. I liked him right away. We talked quite a bit, and one of things that we discussed was that we were both HIV positive. Despite the wasting that Tim was experiencing in his face, he had sparkling green eyes and a confidence that give him a clear charisma. I found out that he was a studied portrait painter, which intrigued me. I told him that I had once been an art teacher. At the end of the evening, in true twenty-first-century fashion, we exchanged e-mail addresses. I went home and promptly did nothing.

I looked at Tim's e-mail address many times over the next few weeks but never wrote to him. I rationalized my behavior with a million excuses, but in the back of my mind I was really thinking, "What if I like him? Then what?"

I had never had a mature relationship as an openly gay man. I didn't know how I would handle it.

Back on the grapevine, I heard that Tim was curious why I hadn't contacted him. Realizing that I didn't come out to sit alone for the rest of my life, I sent the e-mail. We made a date to go to see a movie in South Beach. After the movie, we sat and talked over drinks. We were having a marvelous time, and the evening could have easily ended up at one or the other's apartment, but we decided to take things slow. Both of us felt that this connection was strong enough that we should give a relationship a fair shake and not mess it up with the usual lust thing.

During the weeks ahead, we would meet frequently on Lincoln Road near Tim's house. He had an apartment and studio in the design district—Wynwood—where a lot of local artists lived. We would visit galleries, go shopping, dine at a lot of cool restaurants. Another thing we had in common was eating—we loved good food. We both loved the outdoors and the beach. We joined the same health club and started working out together. With time, we began spending the night at each other's apartments, and the relationship progressed from friendship to something more. Eventually, when I wasn't with Tim, I found myself wondering where he was and what he was doing. We would often call each other just to have the, "What are you doing—nothing—what about you?" conversation.

When I met Tim, he was very thin and still had some medical problems. He was one of the earliest people to contract HIV back in the early 1980s, before the medication was very advanced. In fact, the medicine that he was taking in the early stages of his diagnosis caused him to have a heart attack. As a result, he needed to get a pacemaker implanted, which he still wears today.

Early on in our relationship Tim showed me a documentary that he was in called *The Lazarus Syndrome* about the early days of AIDS. In the film, Tim was very sick and extremely wasted looking. As I watched the documentary, hearing his story moved me tremendously. He has a painting that he did of himself in New York when he was at his worst. It epitomizes what I believe the virus looks like inside you.

Tim depicted himself so disturbingly—and he was obviously so freaked to paint something like this—that the image of him actually made me cry. It also made me look back and say, "If this man has so much character that he can survive this, he can survive anything." This took my respect and feelings for Tim to the next level.

Looking at him today, you would never know all that he has been through. Tim takes very good care of his body and looks great. He's muscular and healthy looking. When someone compliments his body, I want to scream, "Hey, look at me." I still walk slowly from the injury to my knee that I suffered when I was hit by the car. I say to Tim, "I'm like the sun and you're like a little planet buzzing around me. I can never catch up. Slow down."

It's really amazing how far he's come, but the fight against this disease is a constant theme in both of our lives. Tim still has complications that need constant attention, and we know the battle isn't over. But we take it one day at a time and hope for the best. On most days, that's enough.

Early in our relationship, Tim and I had a chance to work together on an AIDS-related project. WMGK—a radio station in Philadelphia—was holding the "102.9 WMGK Classic Rock Art Show" to benefit the Elizabeth Glaser Pediatric AIDS Foundation. The idea of the show was to auction off original art and handwritten, autographed song lyrics from rock musicians and songwriters. I was asked to contribute an original piece of artwork. At first, I hesitated because I hadn't painted in many years. But Tim encouraged me to give it a try.

Tim is wonderful portrait artist. He paints in oils. When I first saw his work, I said "Okay, I'm a little 'a' artist, you're a capital 'A' artist."

The two of us put our heads together and created a painting that we auctioned off for the Elizabeth Glaser Pediatric AIDS Foundation. Tim stretched the canvas, and I painted the AIDS red ribbon on a light gold background. He helped me with the gold leafing—and it looked great. It was exhibited with all the other paintings in Philadelphia. Tim and I flew up to see it and stayed to watch it sell for quite a bit of money. I was thrilled that my music and my artistic skills could come together in a way that was benefiting such an important cause. It was especially gratifying to do it with Tim.

My relationship with Tim was the first real relationship that I had had since Ron, so many years ago. They say the older you get, the more baggage you bring with you. I suppose this is true, but I really wanted this relationship to work, so I was willing to try to shed some of those bags. I began to recognize how important Tim was becoming to me.

I remember one of the first times that I realized this was at—of all places—Disney World. I had gone to Orlando with a few friends. There we were, a bunch of grown men, running around with mouse ears on and taking silly pictures. When we all went over to the Hard Rock for drinks, in the middle of the festivities, I broke away from the group and called my friend Michael back in Chicago. I said, "Here I am in the best freakin' place—the 'fairiest' place ever—and instead of having fun I'm walking around thinking 'Where's Tim? Where's my partner?'"

Shortly after that awakening, Tim began to have some problems with his sight. The cataracts that had formed in his eyes were progressing to the point that his vision was shadowy. For a portrait artist, this is very frightening. He and his doctor agreed that he would need surgery to correct the problem. Tim was obviously nervous about the surgery. I tried to make him laugh by telling him that when he could see better he might change his mind about me. As the day of the surgery approached, I asked him when we had to be at the hospital. He said, "Oh, you don't have to drive me."

I said, "I don't have to drive you, but I'm going to drive you."

When we got to the hospital and he was waiting to be taken into surgery, he told me, "It's okay. You don't have to wait, Chuck. Go home."

I said, "Are you kidding me? I'm staying right beside you."

I think that experience signaled a turning point in our relationship. For the first time, we knew that we weren't going to run away from each other if times got tough. In my opinion, when you love someone, if that person has a problem, you have a problem. No excuses. I was always there for my family, but this was the first time that I made that same commitment to another man. When Tim came out of surgery, the recovery room nurse told me that the first thing he said was, "Where's Chuck?"

I was right outside.

CHAPTER FIFTEEN

REWRITING HAPPILY
EVER AFTER

When I first started treatment for AIDS, at the depths of my physical and emotional despair, my doctor told me, "In five years, you won't recognize yourself. You have no idea how different your life will be."

I don't think even he knew how true those words would prove to be. At the time the thought of it taking years, as opposed to weeks or months, for me to begin feeling better and getting my life back on track was depressing. In retrospect, though, it was all part of the journey. And now, having gone through so much, I felt stronger and happier than I ever had in my life. Physically, I was getting stronger every day and taking great care of my body. Emotionally, I was in my first mature, honest, open relationship with another man. And professionally, I was playing with Styx on my own terms. I wasn't hiding anything from the other band members or from my fans and it felt wonderful.

I wasn't well enough to perform every date on a tour with Styx, so I played on a scaled-back schedule. Traveling that extensively still took too much out of me. Trying to stick to a regular schedule of eating, sleeping, and taking my meds was almost impossible, and after five or six days I would end up getting frazzled. Touring is hard even for a healthy person, but for someone with a compromised immune system, it can be life threatening.

There are things that you never think about when you're healthy.

For instance, when I'm traveling between time zones, when do I take my meds? Sticking to a strict every -n^{th} hour schedule could mean that I would end up having to set my alarm clock in the middle of the night just to take a pill. And if I need to eat something before a show in order to take my meds, I'm always wondering, "Will this upset my stomach while I'm out on stage?" Gastrointestinal disturbances are common with my medication, and even drinking water can sometimes send me running for a bathroom. Despite all the obstacles, however, I still wanted to play as many concerts as I could, and gave 100 percent each time I got on stage. Generally, whenever I played, I felt great—energized and alive.

I think it's also healthy to be out in the world, meeting fans, and interacting with the band and the support crew. Many of the roadies and production techs have traveled with the band for years and I consider them friends. The people behind the scenes are often overlooked but are no less important to the success of a great band. One of these people is George, our tour manager for thirty years.

George is a very smart, very nice man. I used to call him the oldest Boy Scout in the class. He was always very supportive of me during my illness. He and his wife would frequently call to see how I was doing during the dark days when I first started my drug treatments. Of course, since I was so ashamed of my illness and embarrassed over how I looked, I never let them come to visit. I would say, "No, that's okay George, please don't come." Like all the other people I shut out during that period, I now regret my decision. It would have done me good to see their smiling faces.

One day on the road, George and I went to the airport together. We were on the way to our next tour date. Knowing that the bus could be grueling for me, George sometimes made arrangements for me to fly. This time, he was treating me even better. He wanted to use some of his frequent flyer miles to get me upgraded to first class. We went up to the reservation desk and spoke to the attendant. Like most airlines, they only allowed upgrades for family members. We were promptly denied. Just as George was about to thank the woman and walk away, I interrupted.

I put my arm around George and said, "Oh, it's okay. We're domestic partners."

The woman didn't know what to say. We got our upgrade.

I said, "It's okay, George, I won't tell anyone."

But how could I resist such a great opportunity to tease a Boy Scout? That weekend, when the group was together backstage before the show, I said, "Excuse me everyone, I have an announcement. George and I have decided to become domestic partners. But if anything happens, he can still keep Mary and the kids." George was ready to strangle me.

I said, "Oh, come on, George. You have the best job in rock 'n' roll. You have me and your wife."

I had missed these silly moments on the road. They were good for the soul.

After one show in April 2004, I was feeling particularly good. The crowd had been amazing, my energy was flowing, and I was reveling in the post-show high. When we all got on the bus to go home, I stood up and made a grandiose proclamation. I told the guys, "I want you to know that I'm feeling the best that I have in years, and I want to do as much of the tour as I can."

Maybe I tempted fate. A few days later, I visited the doctor for a routine checkup. About a week later, the doctor's office called and said that they needed to see me right away. I called Tim immediately. I told him, "I know what they're going say. My father died of cancer at fifty-six. I'm fifty-six. I know I have it."

He tried to comfort me until we could make it into the doctor's office the next day. When I went back, the doctor told me that my prostate-specific antigen (PSA) numbers had been rising—a possible indication of prostate cancer. He said that they had a reached a level where he thought I should have a biopsy performed.

In my mind, he could have just announced me dead on the spot. Because of the parallel with my father, I was probably more freaked out by this news than I was by my initial diagnosis of HIV. But with Tim's support and reassurance, I went in for all the suggested tests and waited. When the results came back, they showed that I had stage II prostate cancer—not the worst, but still no guarantee of a complete recovery. I had two tumors on my prostate. Because of the drugs that I was on, radiation, seeds, or any of the less invasive treatments were not an option for me. The doctor was recommending radical surgery that could lead to impotency and incontinence. Hmmm, that didn't sound good. Obviously, I was horrified and scared. I also could not believe that after surviving so much in my life God still wasn't through with me. But at least I had a lot of practice at beating the odds.

Eager to find an alternative to surgery, I investigated some stories that I had heard about a physician in Miami who was pioneering a procedure called high-intensity frequency ultrasound. Actually a friend of mine who was a lawyer managed to put me in touch with this doctor. I was thrilled with what he told me about the safety and effectiveness of this new procedure. Unfortunately, the FDA had not approved the procedure yet, so it wasn't performed in the United States, but it was performed in many other countries, including the Dominican Republic. After doing my research, I was willing to take a gigantic leap and scheduled the procedure.

Tim and I flew to the Dominican Republic on a Thursday night and I had the procedure done on Friday. When we went to the clinic, another American man was also there to have the procedure. I went first. Tim held my hand the whole time. When I was in the recovery room Tim heard the man and his wife say to the doctor, "We know Chuck is HIV positive—is there any chance that I'll get HIV because I'm going in after him?"

I'm glad I didn't hear it at the time. Despite my weakened condition I think I would have jumped off the table and pummeled him for his stupidity.

On that Saturday night, the Dominican doctor who performed the treatment organized a special dinner for Tim, the American couple, and me. When I walked into the restaurant, I was amazed.

I said to Tim, "I can't believe it, they're playing a Styx song."

He gave me a weird look. "And why do you think they're doing that?"

I looked up and everyone at my table was standing, smiling, and waving. I said, "Oh. I get it."

We flew back to Miami on Sunday. I never spent one day in intensive care. There was no surgery. There was no downtime at all. Even better, the cancer is completely gone. This was the most amazing twenty-first century medicine that I have ever experienced. Once again, somebody cut me a break. This second brush with death only strengthened my resolve to make the most out of whatever time I have remaining.

About a year after we met, Tim and I decided to take our relationship to the next level and move in together. My condo was a little too small and didn't allow Tim's pug dog, so I moved into his place. This was a big step for me. Living together with another person, particularly at this stage in my life, was challenging. After years of thinking about me, me, me, it was hard to begin thinking of someone else's needs too. I came to the realization that I still had a lot to learn about relationships. Tim had had more experience in this area than I did. He had been in serious relationships in the past. But to his credit, he was willing to work through the hard parts together.

We began building a life together. Despite the occasional growing pains, it was actually quite refreshing to finally be in a loving, committed relationship. Our days were filled with the unremarkable comings and goings of any other couple: "What do you feel like tonight, honey, pasta or chicken?" But to me, having never been in this type of relationship before, this domestic banality was comforting.

There was one glitch in our domestic bliss though. As I mentioned, Tim lived in the Wynwood section of Miami, a neighborhood with a large community of artists, but also a community in transition. Despite all the artists who chose to live here, the streets themselves offered no aesthetic beauty, at least not to my eye. There was garbage littering the sidewalks and graffiti on the buildings. With both of us being such visual people, I didn't feel that living in this environment was healthy for our minds or spirit. Outside of our building, there was a little bodega with a crowd of regulars drinking beer and blasting Salsa music. I was afraid to walk the dog at night and felt like an outsider in my own neighborhood. I was becoming quite reclusive, and one day I said to Tim, "I need to live in a neighborhood where I can walk down the street and say 'hi' to my neighbors."

We agreed to start thinking about a move.

Shortly thereafter, my friend Michael from Chicago was considering moving to southern Florida and was looking in the Ft. Lauderdale area, about forty-five minutes away. He was out one afternoon with a realtor and called me from his cell phone. He said, "Chuck, you have to see this house that I'm standing in. You'll love it." Tim wasn't as anxious to move as I was, but I convinced him to just go and "look."

The house was fantastic. As soon as Tim and I saw it, we both agreed that it was time for a change. It was a modern-style home with marble floors, a swimming pool, and koi pond—quite a change from the urban frontier where we were living. But what I loved even more was the neighborhood. The area is called Wilton Manors, and while there are all kinds of couples and singles living in the area, it also has a very large gay community with many gay-owned shops, restaurants, and businesses. We were sold.

I found my neighborhood where I could say "hi" to the neighbors. In fact, coincidentally, a woman who owned a shop in Chicago that I used to go to also owns a store down the block from us called *We're Everywhere*. When I walked into the store for the first time and saw her, I couldn't believe my eyes. This started a domino effect. Within days I found out about another store owned by a group of gay men from Chicago, and eventually I had met a whole series of friends of friends from the Midwest.

I had never lived in such an open, accepting community—and it felt wonderful. It felt like I'd finally come home. I hope that every young gay person, or anyone who feels that they do not belong in their world, can learn from my experience. There are places where you will be welcomed and people there who will accept you for exactly who you are. Seek them out. It can make all the difference in your life.

While Chicago will always have a special place in my heart, this is now my home. I've begun to put down roots here. I have a house, a beautiful yard, three dogs, and of course, Tim. There's always a cacophony of barking, workers coming and going from the house, telephones ringing, dogs falling in the pool. It's quite a different environment than my pristine condo back in Chicago. But when I'm out traveling with the band, I can't wait to get home to all this madness. I love my life and I have never been happier with all aspects of my life.

My relationship with Tim is challenging and fun and wonderful. He's always in my thoughts even when I'm on the road. That's especially nice since at one time there was no one to think about and no one to share my life. I can finally express myself openly and as a gay man, and I have the kind of relationship that everyone deserves. After decades of self-reproach, I'm actually at the point where I feel that I deserve it. For so many years I didn't think I deserved anything.

Living with HIV is a big part of our lives. We are dedicated to our health because we have to be. We watch what we eat. We work out. We take our medication. I want people to know that staying healthy is a struggle every day. My fear is that people will look at us and think that because we look good, we can't be that sick. This drives my commitment to promote AIDS education and preach the importance of safe sex, HIV testing, and continuing AIDS research. The new HIV drugs are saving lives, but AIDS is still profoundly affecting the lives of millions of people around the world. I know; I live it every day.

Things can still change and go wrong with our conditions. Not only is the protocol very demanding, but the drugs can stop working as effectively over time. The good news at this point for me is that my HIV level is undetectable. I've come a long way. My doctor once told me that some of his patients say that they were glad in some ways that they got HIV because it's such a life-changing experience. I can't say that I'm happy I contracted the disease, but I will admit that it has the power to change you in a positive way. For instance, I don't think my priorities have ever been clearer.

There's the expectation that if something happens to Tim, I'm there for him. Period. And if something happens to me, he's there for me. Tim and I get our blood checked together each month and hear the results in the doctor's office. I have told Tim, "I will never leave you because of your health. I committed to you knowing that your condition is worse than mine. If we ever break up, it will be because we don't want to be together anymore for some other reason, but it will never be about our conditions."

Illnesses like this teach you to live every day in the moment, because you just don't know what the next moment has in store for you.

CHAPTER SIXTEEN

FACES OF VICTORY

I am at a wonderful place in my life now. But whenever I think that maybe it's time to just sit back and relax, and perhaps trade in my public life for a more private existence with my family and friends, something happens to show me why I need to continue. Obviously, my life as a priest didn't work out too well, but nonetheless, God seems to have given me the vehicles necessary to spread compassion and healing in the world. And in the end, I think I see his plan for me. Writing this book offers one platform to tell my story and help those struggling with self-acceptance, or illness, or any other life struggle. My work with the band is another platform.

As I mentioned, it's difficult for me to travel extensively with the band due to my ongoing health issues. It's also hard to travel extensively and maintain my home life with Tim. Spending weeks or months on the road is taxing on a relationship, and it also leaves all the responsibilities of managing a home on the person left behind. I have a new understanding of how hard it must have been on the guys in the band who were married during the years when we toured for months on end.

Tim has come out with me on a few dates, but that brings its own set of problems. When one person is working and the other is not, there's still a lot of time spent apart—it's just being apart in the same city. I think the key is to find ways to stay connected while I'm traveling and reassure Tim that he's always on my mind no matter what city I happen to be sleeping in that night.

Despite the difficulties, I plan on doing as many dates as possible with the group in the coming years. For one thing, the dynamics within the group today are better than ever. I've never felt freer to be myself on stage. Tommy and JY have matured into tremendous musicians and tremendous people. And the "new" members of the group—Todd, Lawrence, and Ricky are not only talented but very nice guys. It's sad that John is not sitting behind the drums, and it's unfortunate the way things ultimately worked out with Dennis, but in other ways this is the Styx of my dreams. Finally, I feel our performances are all about the music and not about the egos. It's extremely cool—we're all having a great time out there.

What still surprises me is how many Styx fans come up to me after the shows to shake my hand, or tell me how good it is to see me back up onstage. When I first started performing again after my illness, I thought the fans might think less of me. It turns out that the opposite is true. At times like these I realize that I can make, and perhaps have made, a difference in helping to spread understanding about a disease that affects millions of people.

Some of the stories I hear on the road just break my heart. Last year we were playing out in the Southwest at an Indian casino. After the show, there were a group of fans who were waiting outside for us to sign autographs. The crowd was small enough that I agreed to sign the usual array of concert programs and CDs. If the crowd is too large, sometimes I just shake hands because it gets too unmanageable to sign every autograph without leaving anyone out. But for a few people it's usually just easier to sign them than to say no. In the midst of all the commotion, a man stepped up to me and said, "Chuck, it's chilly out here. Do you want a sweatshirt?"

I said, "No, I'm okay, thanks."

He didn't give up, insisting that I take one. I looked down and noticed that he had a trunk of sweatshirts with him—he must have been a vendor or something—so I said, "You're right; it is cold."

I was fine, but I thought, "Okay, free sweatshirt, why not."

After the crowd broke up, we all went back to the tour bus to chill out. We were having some drinks and looking at the photos that our photographer had taken of the group that day. Suddenly, there was a knock on the door. The tour manager went over to see who it was, and then turned back to me. He said, "Someone wants to see you, Chuck." I thought, "Great, someone wants another autograph. I knew I shouldn't have started signing them."

I stuck my head out the door, and there was the young man who had given me the sweatshirt. I stepped outside, and said "Hello?" He looked nervous.

"Sorry to bother you. I just wanted to compliment you on your courage for going back out on the road. I know there must be issues . . . you're an inspiration." He looked down at the ground and shuffled his feet a little. "I also wanted to tell you that I've recently been diagnosed with HIV too."

He didn't have to say anything else. I could hear the fear in his voice and see the pain on his face. I knew he must have been suffering.

I said, "I think that you should give me a great big hug."

We embraced, and I asked him to tell me how he was feeling. He told me about the guilt, the fear, the shame—all the things that we all go through when first diagnosed. I gave him this advice, "Forget the shame. Forget the guilt. Those words are not in your vocabulary anymore. There is nothing to be ashamed of here—you did nothing to deserve this illness. It happens. It's a disease. And don't be afraid. There is medicine out there. Six years ago, I felt the same way you do, and I'm here today. And you're much healthier than I was. You're going to do just fine."

We hugged again, and I gave him my e-mail address in case he ever wanted to talk.

When I got back on the bus, I shared my experience with the group. I told them that I just had an incredible encounter with a stranger who had opened up his heart. I think the story even touched the hearts of a bunch of seen-it-all, done-it-all rockers. It felt wonderful that I could help to ease this young man's suffering. This story underscores why I love to go out and perform. I also know that for every person who has the courage to approach me, there are probably ten more out in the audience who are going through the same thing.

Many fans reach out to me through my website www.chuck panozzosplace.com, as well. These e-mails truly touch me, and offer tremendous encouragement and motivation to keep me going out and spreading the word. Here are a few of the hundreds of inspirational notes that I have received.

Chuck,

My respect and admiration for you has grown even greater in the past few months. I start volunteering with my local AIDS Network next week and have you to thank for the inspiration to finally just DO it. Here's to many, many healthy and happy days ahead! Enjoy the sun!!

Chris from Wisconsin

Chuck,

In the 1980s, I had the opportunity to meet you and John at a video shoot for the band. I will never forget how genuine you both were. I have lost many a dear friend to AIDS and know what courage and strength you now possess. Seeing you step forward in this cause, strong and with a great sense of humor, makes my heart joyful. Thank you, Chuck, for being who you are, sharing your true self with us and your limitless talent. May the angels keep you healthy as you teach us all to be better humans.

Vicki from California

Chuck,

As a member of the theatre community, while not a gay man, I have seen oh so many of my friends in the gay community struggle to just live day to day. I have a friend of Middle Eastern descent who cannot come out to his family as his dad is a priest, and from Fiji and openly critical of gays and lesbians. What an inspiration you are, as what greater spotlight can there be than that of a gay rock star in a hetero world! I hope people see you as an example of a man who came out in the hardest of circumstances and is happier than ever!

Good Luck!

A Rabid Styx Fan!

Chuck,

I am a musician who has grown up with your music. (I even played in a Styx tribute band.) As great a bassist as you are, it does not compare to your courage and humanity. You continue to make your own special music. You are a positive influence in a world so often filled with negativity. What you did with Styx was wonderful, what you're doing now will be your legacy . . . good luck and God Bless.

Jim from Concord, New Hampshire

Chuck,

Best wishes. As my Art Teacher at Fenger High School, you taught me to have great courage, and with any great struggle is a great reward. The strength you gave me then, I am glad I can now return. Best Wishes. I will remember you always.

Your Friend,

Bill from Tinley Park, Illinois

Chuck,

Having lived in nearly pathological fear of HIV for years, then my worst nightmare confirmed, and the subsequent months of profound fear and depression, I emerged with new found Hope and Enlightenment. A dear and brilliant friend remarked; "The Universe (read Higher Power) gives you what you need to learn, to grow." Perhaps he was right. I no longer fear HIV. Things once of great importance now are insignificant. Priorities changed and a personal journey began. In an extraordinary and unexpected way, HIV has been a gift. It has taught me many lessons: Lessons of Hope, lessons of Choice, and to learn to love oneself, and appreciate all Things. When we leave this place, we are remembered by our deeds and character not by the car we drove, the neighborhood we lived in, or the balance in our checking account. I can't imagine anything sadder than nearing the end of our journey and looking back with regret. Hopefully, what the world gave us did in fact teach us those lessons we needed to learn, and that has made all the difference.

Best Wishes,

Tim from Minneapolis

Hi Chuck :-)

I just read your story. WOW! I have been a Styx fan almost since the beginning. I remember my brother (he passed away in 1989 from complications due to AIDS) watching a Styx videotape with me when he was very ill. He had started liking Styx through those videos and tapes. When I read your story, it made me remember my brother Edgar. I know this may not sound right but I am glad that you were diagnosed when AIDS research was beginning to produce medications to help those with the disease. My brother was diagnosed during the early days of AIDS and he suffered a lot of pain through many years. I am glad you are and will continue to be a survivor. I will keep you in my heart and prayers. I will be brave enough to admit that when I was a young girl, I had a crush on you! But now that childhood crush is a deep admiration for your strength and bravery. It is a pure and heartfelt love for who you are inside.

YOUR FAN NOW AND FOREVER,

Grace from New York,

Chuck,

I just wanted to let you know that you've been a great inspiration to me. Thanks to your example I have slowly been coming out to friends and certain family members about my bisexuality. I have never felt happier and more accepted—each and every one has been nothing but supportive.

I probably would never have gotten the courage to do this if not for the example you have given. I thank you for the gift of teaching me to be myself. I post this openly instead of privately in the hope that someone else will take the first few steps and see just how freeing it is. You've started something Chuck!

Marni from Orlando, Florida

Chuck,

I hope your efforts in the field of AIDS awareness and true integration of homosexuals in your society will pay off. In my country (The Netherlands) we have had gay marriages for a number of years now, and it's not like we've turned into Sodom and Gomorrah or something like that. Although I'm not gay myself, I've always felt that the whole issue of homosexuality, in the deepest sense of the matter, should not be an issue at all. There is absolutely no reason (other than highly debatable 'religious' motives) to be opposed to gay marriages. If a country does indeed pursue freedom and peace for all, it can only be gained from doing that. In fact, I believe (and I also heard this from friends who are gay), in some quiet way, the impact of legalizing gay marriages was so great that it almost wiped out the entire issue. Recently, the gay movement, united under the COC, declared that all major goals have been attained and that there is no longer discrimination in an institutional, legal, and social sense.

I also believe that legalizing gay marriages has contributed to AIDS awareness and acceptance of those who suffer from it. The notion that AIDS is typically a disease for homosexuals is no longer present here. Of course, there are exceptions, and the gay movement still remains alert, but the battle for full institutional and social recognition has been won and no longer exists. Public information about AIDS and its consequences is now directed toward everyone in general, just like every other disease.

So once again, I think the issues you are involved in are very worthy causes and I really hope you will succeed. The effects will be purely positive to each and everyone.

Let me finish by saying that I'm very grateful for the fact that I can communicate with you, here today in 2005. Your courage and willpower in fighting various serious illnesses and life's hardest moments is a true inspiration to me. And from yet another selfish point of view, I think it's a joy I can continue listening to you making wonderful music.

With the highest respect and warmest regards,

Jools

I think it's fitting that I end this book with a story about someone who has become very special to me. His name is Dylan Rice and he is a young, very talented musician. He is also gay. Several years ago, in 2003, I had the pleasure to meet Dylan. Since then, we have formed a very special relationship. I'd like to think that I am something of a surrogate, older gay brother to him. But in reality, I'm sure he would point out that I'm more in the age range of surrogate uncle. Oh, well— either way I hope that I have been something of an example to Dylan—a mentor on how to be true to oneself within the larger context of the music industry. My life can also serve as an example of what not to do. I've certainly made my share of mistakes and I hope a younger generation can learn from these. I didn't have any mentors within the business when I started. Perhaps that's why my friendship with Dylan is so important to me.

I first met Dylan on a fluke. In addition to his music career, he was doing freelance work as a writer for *Poz* magazine to make ends meet. *Poz* is a magazine that focuses on men living with HIV. They wanted to do an interview with me about how I was coping with HIV, and I said yes. When the reporter called me, it was Dylan. Right away we hit it off. Dylan told me that he also worked for Chicago's Department of Cultural Affairs and booked many of the entertainers and musical events at the Chicago Cultural Center, which was right down the street from me in Chicago. He also told me that he was a musician. He asked if we could get together in person to do the interview. I agreed, and we met for coffee.

During the interview, we talked about my life and the challenges of living with HIV. We also talked about music. Every time we tried to focus on the interview, the conversation seemed to keep flowing back to Dylan's guitar playing or my experiences with Styx. Obviously, we had a very strong common interest. Dylan told me that ultimately he wanted to become a full-time musician. I told him to keep at it, and told my story of working as a teacher, then spending years struggling on the road before I was able to make enough money to live comfortably as a musician.

When the interview was over, we exchanged cards and kept in touch. We seemed to bond very quickly and had a mutual respect for each other's talents. The next time that Styx was performing in Chicago, I invited Dylan to come see us perform. He came to the show. I think it was cool for him to watch Tommy introduce me and see the support that the audience showed for me. I, in turn, went to see Dylan perform with his band and was blown away by his talent.

Like me, Dylan was also the only gay member of his band. Unlike me, Dylan has been very open about his sexual orientation with his band mates. They all know and support his commitment to the gay community. Dylan and his group often perform at gay-related benefits and fundraisers. It's a different time than when I started out in the industry, and it makes me very happy and proud to see Dylan embracing his true self so openly in the music world. Watching Dylan's career grow gives me hope that things are getting better for gay musicians.

Shortly after Dylan and I became friends, his band had the opportunity to play at a gay and lesbian music festival called, "Queer Is Folk Festival" at the Old Town School of Folk Music in Chicago. It is organized annually by another Chicago-based out musician, Scott Free. Dylan surprised me by asking if I would like to perform with them. I was touched, and I thought it would be a kick, so I agreed.

When we began rehearsals, it was like a flashback to the early days of Styx. In addition to Dylan as lead singer and guitar, Matt Neuroth played guitar, Jon Van Bladel played drums, and Cory Hance sang backup vocals. We all crammed into in a crappy little rehearsal studio somewhere in Chicago, just like John, JY, Dennis, and I had done so many years ago. The guys kept apologizing to me for the setup, but I said, "Are you kidding, there is no need to apologize. This is great. You're taking me back. I should be thanking you."

The rehearsal went well. We all jammed and I think the other guys enjoyed playing with me. Afterward, we all went out for hot dogs and beer. It was cool.

When the day of the performance came, we all went to the museum. It was like the Ted Mack amateur hour. Also, as a folk concert, it was supposed to be all acoustic, but somehow we managed to worm our way in with electric instruments. I looked around at the other performers with their acoustic guitars and said, "Dylan, you realize we're going to blow these people away. We have amps!"

We performed one of Dylan's songs called "Barely Knew You," then we did "Come Sail Away." When I looked out at the audience, I was surprised and really touched to see one of the nurses from the clinic that I had gone to when I was so sick. The crowd went wild for us. There was a huge round of applause. I knew from the response that we had something powerful going on.

After that day, we played together a few more times at parties and other informal events. Then in 2006, I was asked to be a Champion for the Gay Games in Chicago. The Gay Games is a sporting competition that attracts gay and lesbian athletes from around the world. I was honored to be asked to participate. I was also honored when Dylan announced to me that he wanted to write a song for the games and perform it together at the event. I saw this as a historic opportunity for two gay musicians to perform together in their hometown of Chicago at the Gay Games. We wouldn't be there because we were runners or swimmers or high jumpers, but because we were musicians. Somehow I saw this as coming full circle—two generations of gay men, two very different experiences, yet sharing a common bond.

I have the opportunity to tell Dylan personally how proud I am of him. But I know that there are other young people out there who may feel disenfranchised, who do not have anyone encouraging them or telling them to not to deny who they are. I hope I can be that person, if only through my words and my music.

Dylan and I performed the song "Faces of Victory" at the closing ceremony of the Gay Games last summer. Here are the beautiful lyrics that Dylan wrote. May they offer you inspiration and hope.

THE FACES OF VICTORY
BY DYLAN RICE

Now's the moment, take my hand, talk a walk with me
Brother, sister, come together with dignity

We are the face
We are the faces of victory
And we shine our name for the world to see and believe
We made a place
We made a place in history
Just by being here, no apologies, you and me

We will fight just to love, we will love even though we fight
We will fight just to love, we will love even though we fight

From the shadows, from the veils of secrecy
come the people: We are many, and still growing

We are the face
We are the faces of victory
And we shine our name for the world to see and believe
We made a place
We made a place in history
Just by being here, no apologies, you and me

We will fight just to love, we will love even though we fight
We will fight just to love, we will love even though we fight

We are the face
We are the faces of victory
It's our time—we're catching up, Love

LESSONS LEARNED

People may think that because I have achieved a certain degree of fame and success in my life that I may have escaped some of the negative stigma and discrimination that goes along with being gay. After all, it's showbiz. Everyone is gay, right? It doesn't matter. I think there will always be a prejudice in show business toward gay performers until society at large changes its perceptions toward gay men and women. When you're trying to market yourself to the public, whether as a gay actor, athlete, or rock star, you can't help feel the unspoken pressure to keep your sexuality under wraps. If you're after mass appeal, gay doesn't always sell in Peoria.

Examples of this still abound. Not long ago there was a story in the news about an out, gay actor—Chad Allen—who was cast to play a Christian missionary in the movie *End of the Spear*. There was a big brouhaha from the Conservative Right because he was a gay man playing a real-life religious martyr. Ultimately, he was still given the role. It is just a shame, however, that actors like Allen, who are brave enough to stand up for who they are, still have to go through this kind of prejudice. It is also not surprising that some famous actors rumored to be gay, but not yet out, still feel that they have to hide their sexuality in order to be successful.

Television can be even more homophobic. There was recently an ABC reality show called "Welcome to the Neighborhood" where several families competed to win a house in a conservative neighborhood in Texas. Two gay men and their adopted son ended up winning a house. Two weeks before the series was supposed to air, ABC abruptly pulled the show. It was speculated that they did this under pressure from four powerful religious groups that had recently pledged their support to ABC/Disney's new movie, The Chronicles of Narnia. These religious groups had only recently lifted a ban against Disney for supporting gay tourist weekends in its theme parks, and ABC didn't want to rock the boat.

It seems obvious that their decision was all about money. It's unfortunate, because this particular show could have exposed many people to a responsible, loving gay family. By showing gay families as regular people who could be your neighbors, members of your church, or simply your friends, ABC had the opportunity to change millions of perceptions, and they blew it. Sometimes the only exposure that the general public has to gay people is through the media's coverage of events like pride parades. And while these events are important, they often feature over-the-top exhibitions of gay pride. This is not real life, and it's important to show that most gay men don't wear feathers to work everyday.

It is true that homophobia is also common within the world of rock. But when you consider the level of homophobia that pervades our society, I suppose I didn't suffer any more, or any less, discrimination than any other gay man or woman, regardless of profession. But that's still too much. Even after all this time, I am often startled at the insensitivity shown toward the gay community. For the most part, I believe that much of this insensitivity is the result of ignorance. As a former teacher, I realize the importance of knowledge. It's the only way to eradicate the prejudice and intolerance that we face every day. Generally, in my own life, when I have had the courage to take a stand and confront the issue head-on, the offending party is almost always surprised and regretful.

Fortunately, I am now comfortable enough in my own skin to take a stand on my own behalf. But I know that there are thousands of others who are not. For them, I hope to be an example. For them, I hope to help break down the stigma and stereotypes that still surround not only the gay community but also many other groups and individuals who feel disenfranchised. For every Pat Robertson, we need someone else to challenge him and ask, "Where did you get your facts?"

Allowing misguided individuals to turn gay issues into their own political agenda can have disastrous consequences for so many people. This is particularly true when these views are extended to the opposition of AIDS research funding. You can't make a judgment call on a disease. It's just wrong. You never hear anyone say, "You got a heart attack because you're too fat, so we're not going to invest in heart research. Or, you got cancer because you smoke, so let's stop the cancer funding." It's illogical. But HIV/AIDS gets caught up in this kind of political nonsense. I also think that Americans forget that AIDS is not only a gay issue. Around the world millions of men, women, and children are dying of this disease. Research that leads to an AIDS vaccine could be one of the most important achievements of this century. And in the meantime, we need to invest in education that will contain its spread.

Even in the gay community, there is still a lack of information on many important issues that affect us every day, including HIV/AIDS. Despite all the information available, there are people who remain as confused as I once was. One time when I was getting my hair cut, the stylist whispered to me, "I have to ask you something. Can I get HIV from having oral sex with someone who is positive?" I said, "Let's put it this way, if you could transmit HIV through oral sex, I think every gay man out there would be positive." But I told him to educate himself! I could not believe that a forty-year-old gay man still hadn't figured it out. It also astounds me that so many gay men are still having unprotected sex, and that so many of these men have never been tested for HIV. I understand that getting tested can be scary, but the fear of not knowing is actually worse than knowing the truth—whatever the results.

There is also a unique problem surrounding the younger generation of gay men and HIV/AIDS. There is currently a whole generation of adult gay men who have no idea what the generation before them went through. They didn't see their friends die like I saw my friends die. It's like telling World War II stories: They think, "The war is over, who cares?" But new infection rates are still too high.

There's a certain culture of young, gay men who continue to go to circuit parties, do drugs, and take way too many chances. There is a feeling that *if*, God forbid, they do contract HIV, they can just take the medicine and everything will be okay. Let me tell you, Tim and I think about our illness every day. It has changed and affects every facet of our lives. The treatment has improved, but it is by no means an easy path, especially since with proper education, it can all be avoided.

The facts are out there, but you have to guide young people. They need mentors and teachers. If HIV/AIDS, or sex education in general, remains a topic that we shy away from, then young people are going to be on their own to figure it out, just like I was so many years ago. But today, it's a lot scarier out there—and a lot more sophisticated. Society throws sex at us from every direction. Through television, videos, song lyrics, kids are exposed to sexual images and suggestions earlier and earlier.

I think it must be difficult growing up today. For gay kids, some things are probably better now than when I was growing up—for instance, there is more information available and a few more role models. However, some things haven't changed all that much. Gay adolescents often still do not have the same opportunities to make the same transitions that their straight friends go through in terms of dating or relationships. Many still feel isolated and different and keep to themselves. And if you don't go to a high school or college that is progressive enough to have gay and lesbian alliances, how do you meet people? The Internet can be dangerous. Connections started at clubs or gay bars often involve drugs or alcohol and go nowhere. I used to say, "Spend all your time hanging out at a gay bar and I guarantee you'll meet the drunk of your dreams." As a group, I know that the gay community has come a long way. But we still have a lot to fight for.

For one thing, I believe we need to make sure that we are protected under the law. The fact that Florida, the state that I live in, outlaws adoption by gay couples is outrageous. There is no basis for this kind of legislation except ignorance. Despite the state's huge gay population, our current elected leaders just don't get it. The fact that thousands of children are tossed around between crummy foster homes when there are gay couples eager to give these children loving homes infuriates me. It should infuriate any thinking person.

Gay marriage is another issue that we need to work toward as a community. For me, the issue of gay marriage has more to do with protection under the law rather than a spiritual commitment. For instance, if something were to happen to me, in the absence of an extremely detailed will, the state could come in and take everything—our home, my assets, all the pieces of the life we built together. Tim would have no rights even though he is my life partner. And what's even scarier is that if Tim or I were admitted to the hospital, we could be denied access to seeing each other because we're not family members. We could end up dying alone in a hospital bed.

Obviously, discriminatory laws like these relegate gay Americans to second-class-citizen status. I believe that most good people, just people, understand this. Of course, some people will never get it. That's why the Far Right tries to create this caricature of us. When you dehumanize a race, or a group, then you can do anything that you want to them. History tends to repeat itself, but over time, things can change.

I've been given the unique opportunity to make a difference. I do not take that opportunity lightly. My commitment to achieving equal rights for all is as important to me as any work I have ever done on stage. And so my work continues. My wish is to inspire others, gay or straight, to live a proud, truthful life. If I can help just one person to follow his bliss, I have changed the future.

Love and Peace to All,
Chuck